D1498379

PAUL AND JESUS

ATS
227
R43

2.10

PAUL AND JESUS

Origin and General Character of Paul's Preaching of Christ

By
HERMAN RIDDERBOS

Professor of New Testament
Kampen Theological Seminary
Netherlands

Translated by
DAVID H. FREEMAN

Associate Professor of Philosophy
University of Rhode Island

PRESBYTERIAN AND REFORMED PUBLISHING CO.
Nutley, New Jersey
1977

7981
10   1462

COPYRIGHT © 1957

BY THE PRESBYTERIAN AND REFORMED PUBLISHING COMPANY

PHILADELPHIA, PA.

Library of Congress Catalog Card Number 57-8807

PRINTED IN THE UNITED STATES OF AMERICA

TRANSLATOR'S PREFACE

In *Paul and Jesus,* Herman Ridderbos, an outstanding New Testament scholar, seeks to understand the preaching of Paul within the framework of the history of revelation. In a sense the book is an introduction to Paul in that it deals with the main perspectives of his preaching and critically compares the latter with the self-disclosure of Jesus.

Although the primary aim of the work is to arrive at a clear understanding of the character of Paul's preaching, the author carries on a continuous polemic with outstanding representatives of New Testament criticism and devotes considerable attention to the position of R. Bultmann, so that the sub-title of *Paul and Jesus* might well have been *Revelation or Myth.*

The Presbyterian and Reformed Publishing Company, under the able leadership of Dr. Samuel G. Craig and his son Charles H. Craig is not only to be commended for undertaking the translation of this work, but also for its ambitious plans to translate two other works by Dr. Ridderbos, one on the history of the gospels and another on the synoptic gospels, *The Coming of the Kingdom.*

The work of translation was greatly aided by the author's correction of the manuscript and by the many valuable suggestions of Dr. Ned Stonehouse. I would also like to express my gratitude to Mr. H. De Jongste, for his assistance with the footnotes; and to Mrs. Lewis Grotenhuis for her patient assistance in preparing the manuscript.

DAVID H. FREEMAN

University of Rhode Island

CONTENTS

PAUL AND JESUS

THE PROBLEM OF "PAUL AND JESUS" IN THE NEW CRITICISM

1. Wrede and the Liberals

The theme often described by the words 'Jesus and Paul' or 'Paul and Jesus' (depending upon whether one begins with the preaching of Jesus or of Paul) has been on the agenda of New Testament theologians for many decades.[1] It is now treated differently, however, than fifty years ago when liberal theology still ruled the field. The theme retains its significance because no one who examines the gospels, especially the synoptic gospels, and then reads the epistles of Paul, can escape the impression that he is moving in two entirely different spheres. The difference has a special relation to the position which the person of Jesus Christ takes in both groups of New Testament writings. The gospels portray Jesus as the preacher of the kingdom of heaven; a person who walked on the hills of Galilee, and gave his commandments in the sermon on the mount. They depict a Jesus who was moved by the fate of distressed sinners; a person who ate with both pharisees and publicans; a man who suffered, died, and penetrated into the deepest depths of human existence. However, when Paul writes of Jesus, as the Christ, all such historical and human traits appear to be obscure, and Christ appears to have significance only as a transcendent divine being. It is true that he enters the fulness of time and descends to earth to take part in the conflict against superhuman powers, and therefore permits himself to be nailed to the cross, and given over to death, but in all this he remains the pre-existent, eternal Son of God. And just as he once had shared divine glory and the divine creative work, he is now again exalted upon the throne of God, and is above everything that has a name in heaven and on the earth. At his feet the whole cosmos is laid; he is the pneumatic head of his church, the future judge of the living and the dead.

As long as theology was willing to bow before the scriptures as the word of God, it was able to express the unity of this two-fold picture in its confession of the humiliation and exaltation of Jesus Christ, as the Son of God. Theology was scarcely interested in the historical development of revelation and in how Paul arrived at his Christological statements. Under the influence of the Enlightenment and the theory of evolution the situation changed, and a new view of Holy Scripture developed. The attempt was made to detach the Jesus portrayed in the synoptic gospels from what was called the cadre of a super-natural world-view. The biblical account of Jesus of Nazareth was no longer viewed as the history of the Son of God, who had descended from heaven, but only as the history of a man, the preacher of an exalted justice . . . and one no longer knew what to do with Paul's transcendent Christology.

No doubt the so-called liberal school, from which the aforementioned picture of Jesus is derived, tried to maintain the unity between Jesus and Paul. The main lines of the procedure according to which it operated can be briefly described. That Jesus was the prophet of the spiritual kingdom of God, of religious optimism, and of rational morality nearly became a dogma. Liberal theologians were fully aware that a tremendous gulf existed between this projected Jesus image of the synoptic gospels and Paul's preaching of Christ (the gospel of John was considered to be of little importance for the knowledge of the historical Jesus). To maintain the unity

between Paul and the synoptics, the liberals then explained
the exalted and divine figure of Christ in Paul's writings as
an absolutization of Jesus' moral personality, under the influence of which Paul must also have come. After Jesus' death
the belief of the disciples considered and proclaimed him
to be the resurrected Messiah, the Lord exalted by God on
high. The disciples connected this faith with all sorts of conceptions of pre-existence and notions of a creation-mediator.
This entire development is to be viewed, however, as a later
theological-mythological formation and transformation of the
deep impression which the moral personality of Jesus had
made upon his disciples. Basically then the liberals accepted
a unity between 'Jesus' and 'Paul.' For the preaching of Paul
in its kernel and main thrust, in spite of all Christological
speculations, was nothing else than the continuation of the
love, hope, and faith which had been preached by Jesus. The
prominent liberal theologians held that Paul's theology is
unacceptable and inaccessible to us. For it obfuscated the
clear light that shone out of Jesus' simple and human preaching. Nevertheless, Paul's religion shared a common origin
with Jesus' preaching. For both can be understood in terms
of a child-like trust in God, and the love of one's neighbor.[2]

This relationship between Paul and Jesus broke asunder
however, under the attack of Wrede whose work initiated
a revolutionary movement in Gospel criticism[3] and in the
treatment of Paul's preaching. In spite of Wrede's rejection
of the gospel of Mark as a basis for the then current description of the life of Christ, he nevertheless remained within
the liberal movement, as far as his conception of the 'historical' Jesus was concerned. However, his sensational publica-
tion *Paul* in 1905 signified a complete break with liberalism.
Wrede no longer recognized an antithesis between Paul's 'religion' and his 'theology' (as in Holtzmann). Wrede main-
tained that Paul's theology is the expression of his religion,[4]
and the very heart of Paul's theology is his Christology. The

entire Pauline doctrine is essentially concerned with Christ
and his work; that is its essence.[5] The real significance of Paul
is that he has made the redemptive facts—the incarnation, the
death and the resurrection of Christ—the foundation of religion.[6] The history of redemption is the heart of Pauline
Christianity.[7] According to Wrede, it is therefore impossible to accept with the *Coryphaei* of the liberal theology
(Holtzmann, Wellhausen, Harnack) that Paul is in truth
the one who had understood the gospel of Jesus. Jesus knew
nothing of that which is for Paul the content of religion.[8]
Paul made religion into a religion of redemption; he sees
Jesus arise as the savior of the world, in a great redemptive
historical drama. Even the doctrine of justification by faith,
to be explained in terms of the struggle against particularistic
Judaism, is only an accidental facet of this basically meta-
physical doctrine of redemption.[9] Paul is thus viewed as the
second founder of Christianity.[10] For the true and original
Christianity, one must go back from the second originator
to the first.

2. *The Religionsgeschichtliche Interpretation*

Wrede's conception of the relationship between Jesus
and Paul opened the door to the interpretation of Paul's
preaching in terms of the history of religion (*religionsgeschichtliche* interpretation). As long as an intrinsic and fundamental unity between Paul and Jesus was accepted—as in
the liberal school—it was then only necessary to explain the
theological scaffolding of Paul's preaching within Judaism
and the religious and mythical conceptions of Hellenism.
After Wrede's relentless criticism, however, it became increasingly difficult to explain Paul's preaching on the basis of the
liberal picture of Jesus. Modern theology continued to hold
(it still does) to its naturalistic conception of the person of
Jesus. But it now felt required to explain the origin of Paul's

peculiar Christology which in effect was considered to be a religion different from and often opposed to that of Jesus. This evaluation of Paul's preaching labeled Christianity as a *syncretism* in the proper and basic sense of the word, and ascribed a central and essential role to the *religionsge- schichtliche* method within New Testament science.

Henceforth the investigation of Paul's preaching was entirely dominated by the *religionsgeschichtliche* science, which underwent a remarkable development at the begin- ning of the twentieth century, and not only did it offer aid in examining what had been previously viewed as eccentric portions of Pauline Christology, but it pretended to give the sole and integral explanation of Paul's religion.

For the New Testament scholar Wrede, for example, the *religionsgeschichtliche* explanation of Paul's proclama- tion of Christ was still in many ways a postulate. To anyone who considers Jesus to be what he really was, i.e., an his- torical human personality, the cleft between this person and the Son of God of Paul can only appear tremendous (*unge- heuer*).[11] Jesus was not dead the length of a human life- time before his stature was not only infinitely increased, but also entirely changed. How did this come about?

According to Wrede it is impossible that this image of Christ could have originated from Paul's impression of the personality of Jesus,[12] or from his conversion experience.[13] Such a view makes the heart of this doctrine of Christ to be a spiritual product of Paul, a work of his fantasy. Only one other explanation remains: Paul believed in such a heavenly being, in such a divine Christ, before he believed in Jesus. Such a conception was already in his mind before he had any knowledge of 'the historical Jesus.' "The Pauline Christ is only intelligible when it is assumed that Paul, as a Pharisee, already had a number of ready-made conceptions of a divine being which he later transferred to the historical Jesus."[14] Wrede apparently cannot specify exactly from

where Paul derived his conception of this divine 'being.'
Wrede mentions that Paul originated from an entirely different 'schicht' of Judaism than Jesus, and he speaks of the
rabbinical wisdom, and the speculation of the *apokalyptici*,
and the sphere (*die Luft*) of Hellenistic ideas.[15] He would also
recognize that Paul could partially derive his faith in Christ
from the so-called early church. He could join with the faith
of the Christians of Jerusalem who as the result of their
'visions' of Jesus' resurrection, considered him to be the
Messiah. Nevertheless, the distance between the conception
of the early church of Jerusalem and that of Paul is very
great. Paul's doctrine concerning Christ is new, not only
because the *man* Jesus signifies much more for the early
church than for Paul, but especially because the origin and
essence of Jesus became something heavenly to Paul.[16]
Wrede wishes to explain this doctrine in Paul in terms of
existing *religionsgeschichtliche* conceptions, even though he
is not able to give any exact description of their origin. This
explanation of the origin of Paul's Christology is clearly a
religionsgeschichtliche postulate.

Gunkel writes in the same vein. He agrees that the
origin of the Pauline and Johannine Christology is not ex-
plicable simply in terms of the tremendous impression of the
person of Jesus, or in terms of Paul's vision on the way to
Damascus, nor in terms of the Judeo-Hellenistic doctrine of
the heavenly primeval image of humanity.[17] Liberal theology was wrong in its notion that this supernatural picture of
Christ, which has cosmic significance, could have been a
projection of Paul's subjective experiences. Gunkel also
accepts the postulate: that this figure of Christ must have
been given to him or had at least been prepared previously.[18]
As to where this conception of Christ originated, Gunkel
finds no parallel within the Old Testament or within Judaism
for such great religious ideas. When Paul speaks of Christ
as a heavenly figure, the image of the invisible God, in whom

lives all fulness of divinity; the first born of all creatures, who
has humiliated himself, and taken on a human form; who
underwent a humiliating death and a glorious resurrection,
and who is glorified by God, and who will quickly come
again to destroy sinful humanity, by the words of his mouth,
then all this must, according to Gunkel, be viewed in connection with alien religions (in which this is all *ganz
geläufig*).[19]   The conception of the heavenly Christ 'must'
already have existed before the New Testament.   Within
the Jewish apocalyptic there are traces indicating that such
a faith already existed within Jewish circles.   Provisionally,
however, we cannot say in which form such a faith had
existed; for there is a great gap here in our knowledge.
Even though nothing appears from the sources of this faith
in Christ within Judaism, we must assume the existence of
such a faith in order to understand the New Testament.[20]
The disciples applied the ideals of their heart to Jesus. These
strange religious motives must have penetrated into the
church of Jesus directly after his death.   Thus, Christianity
is a syncretistic religion.[21]

In Gunkel, even more strongly than in Wrede, the *religionsgeschichtliche* explanation of Pauline Christology appears to rest entirely upon strange motives and elements.
Even such a scholar as Gunkel could not deny his embarrass-
ment in demonstrating the *religionsgeschichtliche* origin of
Paul's Christology.   It is particularly meaningful that Gunkel
calls the origin of the Pauline and Johannine Christology
"The greatest problem in New Testament studies."[22]

At Gunkel's instigation at the beginning of the twentieth century, the *religionsgeschichtliche* school attempted
to explain the origin of Paul's transcendent Christology in
terms of conceptions found in specific segments of the Judaism of Paul's day.[23]   The course quickly changed, however,
and scholars began an intense study of the Greek religiosity
at the beginning of the Christian era.   Two scholars of great

reputation came to the fore: Wilhelm Bousset, who sought the origin of Pauline Christology within the Hellenistic mystical cults, and Richard Reitzenstein, who would find the real origin of the Pauline and Johannine view of Christ within the religious gnosis of the Middle East, i.e., within the Hermetic writings, and within the literary products of Mandaeism and Manicheaism. Although these two methods of explanation do not exclude each other, Reitzenstein appeared to be most influential.

Provisionally, the explanatory key was sought within the conception of the cults of the Hellenistic mystery religions. During the first ascendency of the *religionsgeschichtliche* explanation of Paul's 'theological background,' the impression was sometimes given that Christianity, as proclaimed by Paul, actually was nothing else than a specialization of one of the many mystery religions of the Hellenistic religiosity. Not only was much of Pauline terminology, referring to baptism and the Lord's supper, explained phenomenologically and materially in terms of the Hellenistic religiosity, but so was the central element of Paul's gospel: his preaching of Jesus Christ as the crucified, risen, and exalted Lord. For was there not a cult-myth at the basis of all mystery religions, whether that of the Egyptian Osiris, the Syrian Adonis, the Phrygian Attis, the Thracian Dionysus, or the Persian Mithras? Did they not all contain a story of the adventures of a deity, with which the initiates of these various cults believed themselves to be in contact, in a physical pneumatic communion, and whose divine power of immortality is embraced in all sorts of magical-sacrament ceremonies? And did not all these cult-myths concentrate upon the problem of death? And wasn't there within these cults the notion of a dying and a resurrected deity? Was it not possible to ascertain by closer study, for example, of the Isis mysteries, a clear transfer of the fate of the dying and resurrected deity to the pious that had been initiated within the cult? And did this

not of itself bring to mind the Pauline notion of the believers'
dying with Christ and rising with Christ? Often cited in
this connection are the verses recited at the initiation rites
of the cult of Isis: θαρρεῖτε μύσται τοῦ θεοῦ σεσωσμένου
ἔσται γὰρ ἡμῖν ἐκ πόνων σωτηρία[24] ("Take heart, O initiates!
the deity is saved; for us also salvation is at hand.")

After a period of time, however, the so-called parallels
were unable to make very much impression. Especially
in connection with Christology, the redemptive facts proclaimed by Paul and the Hellenistic mystical cults were so
formally and materially different that one can hardly speak
of parallels, let alone speak of genetic connections. To mention only a few points: whereas Paul speaks of the death and
resurrection of Christ and places it in the middle of history,
as an event which took place before many witnesses, in the
recent past, the myths of the cults in contrast, cannot be
dated; they appear in all sorts of variations, and do not give
any clear conceptions. In short they display the timeless
vagueness characteristic of real myths. Thus the myths of
the cults, even though they speak of the death and resurrection of the deity, for the majority at least, are nothing
but depictions of annual events of nature in which nothing
is to be found of the moral, voluntary, redemptive substitutionary meaning, which for Paul is the content of Christ's
death and resurrection. The power of Christ's death and
resurrection was proclaimed by Paul as a forensic and ethical
emancipation. The entire meaning of the mystery religions
is expressed in the *athanasia*, the conquering of natural death,
the escaping of the power of fate, and the return of the
divine-in-man to its origin and end. Whereas, in the view
of Paul, faith and repentance occupies an indispensable
place, within the mystery religions, it is entirely superfluous,
or insofar as it can be spoken of, it bears an entirely different character: The magical rules everything. Paul speaks
of walking in love, humility, mercy, and good works, whereas

a physical, dualistic world view is at the foundation of the
mystery religions, and salvation is accomplished by the
transfer of a divine vital force, expressed sometimes in
asceticism and at other times in the most unrestrained
libertinism. And we still have said nothing of the cleft between the material employed in the myths of the cults, in
order to portray the re-living of the deity, and the preaching
of the passion, the death, and resurrection of Christ. When
still in 1933 Lietzmann appeals to the Isis mysteries to prove
that the conception of dying with Christ and rising again with
him (Rom. 6, vs. 3, 4), could not have developed out of the
Jewish purification ceremonies, but must be viewed as an
"Hellenistic material,"[25] one must then remember that at the
foundation of the Isis mysteries, the myth of the cult speaks
first of the murder of Osiris, by his brother Seth, after which
his dead body is cut and hacked into pieces. And finally,
when the scattered limbs of Osiris are again brought together, from all directions, the re-living of Osiris takes place,
and his identification with Isis follows. It is no wonder that
the apologist Theophilus of Antioch already made fun of a
comparison of the resurrection of Christ with the re-living of
Osiris, a conception apparently already introduced in his
own time.[26]

The real agreement between Paul's proclamation of
Christ and the Hellenistic piety of the mysteries, according to
Wilhelm Bousset, is not found in the idea of the dying and re-
living deity, but in the essence of the cult itself: the mystical
union with the deity.[27] Paul's Christology is then to be characterized as mystical and pneumatic. "The Lord is the
Spirit and where the Spirit is, there is freedom." According to Bousset, Paul's religion can be summarized in this
expression. Paul's Christology does not move within the
categories of knowledge or history but in those of experience,
feeling, mysticism, and ecstasy. This mystical religiosity,
supposedly derived by Paul from the Greek-Hellenistic com-

munity, found its fertile soil within the pagan conceptions of the cult in Antioch. It could then become the form in which the Jewish messianic faith, and the early Christian dogma of the Son of Man, was transferred into the Greek world.[28] Christ is no longer the historical Jesus or the king sent by God to Israel, or the Son of Man, the judge of heaven and earth. Christ is now the *Kyrios* of the cult, a parallel of the heroes of the cult found in pagan religions. He is the transcendent, supernatural *pneuma*, with whom the initiates unite in a mystical union and thereby escape the material, sensory, historically bound world. Bousset admits, however, that Paul represented the mystical piety of the cult in a more personal manner, and developed it in relationship to the ethical sphere.

Bousset's conception of Paul's Christology is noteworthy because it forms the transition from the rational, ethical view of the Christ of liberal theology to the existentialist thought of our own time. It is a typical spiritual product of the first world war period. People began to get enough of cold modernism, and require that the heart be given its due. The words 'Christ-experience,' 'Christ-mysticism' and 'Christ-fellowship' suddenly appeared everywhere. To this extent one can also say that the *religionsgeschichtliche* school, because of its deeper knowledge of religious life, is more profound than the liberal modernism, which celebrated its highest triumph at the end of the last century. This does not remove the fact, however, that Bousset's explanation of Paul's preaching of Jesus Christ, as the pneumatic *Kyrios*, and his characterization of Paul's religion as mysticism, seeks the origin of Pauline Christology outside of the early Christianity established by Jesus' advent and preaching. Bousset's view is therefore just as speculative as the earlier liberal view. The weakness of the historical foundation of his construction is constantly more clearly demonstrated by criticism itself. That we know little or nothing of the pre-Pauline Christianity

of Antioch, from which Paul is supposed to have derived the
foundation of his Christology, indicates the weakness of the
foundation upon which Bousset built. Moreover, the entire
conception that he derives from the Syrian mystery religion rests more upon conclusions derived from general data
than upon any exact knowledge of the situation. A *fortiori*
this applies also to the *religionsgeschichtliche* postulate employed by Bousset, that the Hellenistic community at Antioch
'must' have joined itself to this veneration of the *Kyrios*.[29]
The facts show that faith in Jesus as the *Kyrios* did not
originate in the Hellenistic community but in the early Jewish
Christian community at Jerusalem.[30] Putting aside this historical aspect, it is of no less significance that Bousset's
characterization of the general character of Paul's Christology
is completely unacceptable. This is even recognized by such
an author as Bultmann, who in many respects follows the
sketch which Bousset has given of the development of New
Testament Christology.[31] Basically, however, Bousset reduces Paul's kerygma to a Christological projection of religious *feeling*, while in fact everything which Paul proclaims
of Jesus Christ is the explication of the unique redemptive
events that occurred in Christ's coming, suffering, death,
and resurrection. Therefore, any interpretation of Paul in
terms of a timeless mystical cult of the Hellenistic religions
can be rejected, without even going into the historical question as to whether Bousset's understanding of such cults is
correct or not. Paul's preaching is relevant to spiritual
life, to putting on the new man, to bringing forth the
fruits of the spirit, i.e., to doing the will of God. But Paul's
preaching does not originate in pagan conceptions of a mystical union with the deity, nor in the mystical, pneumatic
experiences of a cult, in which the pagan *Kyrios* is replaced
by the Christian *Kyrios*. The entire foundation of Paul's
preaching lies rather in the historical revelation of Christ in
the fulness of time, in the intrusion of a new world period,

in the Christocentric fulfillment of the redemptive promise that had been given to Israel.

3. The Eschatological Conception

Especially under the influence of the eschatological explanation of the New Testament, modern theology again recognizes that Pauline Christology is not a projection of universal, religious-moral truths, and it is not the noblest example of a mystical experience of God, such as occurs in so many religions. The heart of Pauline Christology can be understood only if one begins with the *historical* character of the salvation which Paul preached. This new tendency again does justice to the general tenor of Paul's preaching and re-establishes in principle the connection between Jesus and Paul.

The name of Albert Schweitzer is significant here. Both his *Geschichte der Paulinischen Forschung* and his *Die Mystik Des Apostels Paulus* mark a turning point with respect to Paul's preaching. Schweitzer approved of Wrede's criticism of the liberal conception of Jesus and Paul. Schweitzer's own view of the gospels and of Paul differs, however, from that of Wrede. Schweitzer views Paul as the direct continuer of Jesus' work, in the sense that Paul, like Jesus, was entirely dominated by the eschatological dogma of the late Jewish apocalypse. In the case of Jesus, however, the *Eschaton* (and thereby the kingdom and the Messiah), still lay in the immediate future, whereas Paul believed the era of the kingdom had begun with Jesus' death and resurrection. In Paul we therefore encounter a realized eschatology. Schweitzer assumes that Paul begins with a different eschatological scheme than Jesus (e.g., the one occurring in the apocalypse of Baruch and the Fourth Book of Ezra). For Jesus the coming of the kingdom and the Messiah coincided with the end of the world (this is the reason why Jesus considered himself only to be the

Messias designatus) whereas Paul held that the revelation of the messianic kingdom occurred before the entrance of the end of the world.[32] In the messianic kingdom the natural and the supernatural world encounter each other and are united, and the resurrection of Christ signifies for Paul the beginning of the messianic kingdom.

It is of special importance for our subject that Schweitzer would understand Pauline Christology entirely in terms of the expectation of the late Jewish Messiah (the Son of Man). Schweitzer is completely hostile to a *religionsge-schichtliche* explanation. Paul's entire proclamation of Jesus as the Christ is in Schweitzer's opinion simply what could be expected on the basis of Paul's specified Jewish eschatological conception of the Messiah. It is simply the death of Christ and the faith in his resurrection which gives an unknown twist to the eschatological drama. But even in this respect Paul could join Jesus and the early Christian community, since Jesus viewed his own death as the necessary condition for the coming of the kingdom.

It is striking that Schweitzer does not give a clearly defined view of Paul's Christological conceptions. The supernatural character of the person of Jesus Christ in Paul's epistles ought to be explained in terms of the late Jewish conceptions of the Son of Man, and in this connection Schweitzer speaks of the pre-existence of the Messiah. And of Paul's statement in 1 Corinthians 8:6: "One Lord Jesus Christ by whom are all things, and we by him," Schweitzer says that for a person so controlled by the idea of the pre-existence of Christ, the application of the notion of the Logos to Christ as found in John, was easily possible. Moreover the path for the doctrine of the Logos was prepared by the Jewish conception of the works of wisdom and of the word of God. Paul supposedly comes very close to the conception of Logos; witness his pronouncement in 1 Corinthians 8:6. According to Schweitzer, Paul is not interested in whether the value of Christ and the works of the Spirit can be brought into contact with Greek conceptions. Paul was occupied only with the significance of the death and resurrection of Christ for salvation.[33] It is noteworthy how little Schweitzer felt the problem of Pauline and Johannine Christology which Gunkel called the main problem of the New Testament. The reason is partly that Schweitzer does not consider the epistle to the Colossians genuine, in which the cosmic and creative significance of Christ finds its most extensive expression. However, to the extent Paul's Christology contains and depends upon pre-existent, cosmic, and post-existent tendencies, Schweitzer believes, in spite of all *religionsgeschichtliche* theory that he is able to appeal to the Jewish apocalypse as the basis of Paul's eschatology.

Even though Schweitzer's imaginative conception of the tenor of the preaching of Jesus and Paul was not followed in various important details, nevertheless, the general tendency of his work has had a tremendous influence in modern theology. This is true also of the Christological aspect of what had been called the problem of Jesus and Paul.

4. The Synthesis (Bultmann)

The degree to which a new course has been taken can best be demonstrated by examining Bultmann's standpoint on this question. In many ways Bultmann continues the tradition of the liberal and *religionsgeschichtliche* radical criticism, but unlike those theories, Bultmann does not oppose Paul to Jesus. Bultmann agrees with Schweitzer in assuming that the preaching of Jesus and Paul has a common basis within an *eschatological* world view, even though the eschatological situation of Jesus and Paul differ.[34] Jesus looked for the kingdom of God and the messianic office in the future, whereas Paul viewed Jesus' death and resurrection as the arrival of the new era, even though its completion was to take place in the future. From a Christological point of view Jesus' preaching and entry did not yet bear a messianic character, but the power and seriousness with which Jesus spoke of the coming judgment, and the connection that he placed between obedience to his words and the entrance of the kingdom of God, formed the natural foundation and origin of all later Christology. Because Jesus proclaimed with such force the proximity of the judgment, he was in his own person, in his own self, 'the sign of the times,' and he signified in his person the requirement of "Entscheidung" (decision).[35] Even though Jesus did not consider himself to be the Messiah, there is a Christology[36] implicit in his call to repentance and *Entscheidung*. What we find in Paul is, in principle, this Christology, born in the eschatological proclamation and confirmed by the early church's faith in the resurrection. The origin of Pauline Christology is not to be found in the impression of Jesus' high moral personality, nor in Paul's special experience, nor in the mystical piety of Hellenistic cults. It is rather the certainty of the entrance into the eschatological situation in terms of which the Pauline and the entire New Testament theology ought to be explained.

Bultmann very clearly rejects the conception of Bousset and others, because he is of the opinion that they misunderstand the *historical-eschatological* character of Paul's Christology and substitute in its place only the mystical element. Nevertheless, Bultmann remains one of the most prominent advocates of the *religionsgeschichtliche* explanation of the New Testament, and in this respect he cannot agree with Schweitzer insofar as the latter believes Pauline Christology can be reduced entirely to Jewish conceptions of the Son of Man and the Messiah. To explain the Christology of Paul, Bultmann appeals to the general history of religion, particularly to gnosticism. For in the latter, to a greater degree than in mystery religions, redemption is portrayed as a cosmic drama. A redeemer, the pre-existent son of the all highest, his likeness (εἰκών), descends from the world of light to communicate true knowledge, gnosis, to those asleep in ignorance, and at their death to bring them back again as the souls of men. To accomplish his purpose the heavenly redeemer must enter the sphere of enemy powers, and therefore clothes himself in human form. The redeemer must experience and prepare the path by which awakened souls and he himself can return to God. The redeemer must himself be redeemed since by his descent he became subject to the necessities and suffering of earthly existence, so that he must suffer and be persecuted before he can again be exalted to the world of light.[37]

The gnostic myth of the 'redeemed redeemer' with all its fundamental differences from the New Testament, provides for Bultmann a substratum for Pauline and Johannine Christology. Bultmann here agrees very closely with Reitzenstein who in the first two decades of the twentieth century published very extensive studies concerning the mystery religions and gnosticism. Reitzenstein described the gnostic idea of redemption as das iranische Erlösungsmysterium, because the basic form of the gnostic idea of salvation originated in the Persian religion. Besides, since Bousset and Reitzenstein, the independent significance of the gnostic movement has been distinguished more clearly as the supposed basis of the Hellenistic Christian theology, and especially that of Paul and John. The gnostic explanation, especially of Pauline Christology, has gradually placed in the shadows, if not completely submerged,[38] the earlier religionsgeschichtliche reference to the dying and risen deities of the cult-myths of the pagan mystery-religions, and has led to a changed conception of the general character of Paul's (and John's) gospel. For twenty or thirty years much was said of Hellenistic mysticism as the basic form of Paul's preaching of Christ, and for a long time the gnosis was viewed as a spiritual movement of a syncretistic character (composed of pagan and Christian elements). At the present time, following H. Jonas,[39] the *gnosis* is viewed as a general phenomenon of the pre-Christian[40] world of late antiquity. Because of its all-embracing cosmic view of reality (not just a mystical and spiritual view), it was of far-reaching significance for the world view and conceptual material of Christianity, and also of neo-Platonism. The knowledge of this general, pre-Christian *Daseinsverständnis* (i.e., understanding of human existence) of gnosticism is for Bultmann indispensable for an understanding of the New Testament idea of redemption, and particularly of Pauline Christology. The life and world view of gnosticism is also of such great significance because it enables Bultmann to connect Christianity and present day existentialism. In its *Daseinsverständnis* the latter apparently agrees on important points with the dualistic pessimism of pre-Christian gnosticism.[41] It is again evident how much the spirit of the time determines the interpretation of the Scriptures: the 'liberal' Paul of Holtzmann, Harnack, was replaced by the 'mystical' Paul of Bousset, Reitzenstein and others, and now there appears the "existentialist" Paul of Bultmann!

But our present concern is restricted to Christology. Bultmann's views of interest to our theme can be summarized as follows: (a) Paul's preaching of Christ bears an historical-eschatological character and to that extent is in agreement with Jesus and the early Christian community; (b) its further expression and development was influenced very profoundly by the gnostic myth of the 'redeemed redeemer.'

In Bultmann, we thus find a synthesis between an eschatological and a *religionsgeschichtliche* explanation.

Chapter II

JESUS' SELF-REVELATION
AND THE CHRISTIAN KERYGMA

5. *The Person of Christ*

Our sketch demonstrates that the problem of "Jesus and Paul" is in the last analysis a question *of the person of Jesus as the Christ in the kerygma proclaimed by Jesus and Paul.* Undoubtedly, the person of Jesus as the Christ occupies a central place in Paul's preaching, i.e., the person of Jesus is not only the subject but above all is the object and content of the word of God. The main question at issue is therefore whether this was not also the case with Jesus' own preaching.

The liberal conception of Jesus' preaching could not admit the possibility of an affirmative answer. As long as the kingdom of God proclaimed by Jesus was considered to be solely of a religious and moral nature, the person and work of Jesus could in a material sense only fill the role of a great preacher and example within the kingdom of God. And Jesus could only be the founder of this new religion. Sooner or later the origin of Paul's preaching of Christ, as the Son of God, descended from heaven, had to be sought in a religious 'field' different from the one in which the historical Jesus of Nazareth moved.

The new eschatological wing of radical criticism is in this respect an improvement. It at least has in its favor that it has again clearly learned to distinguish the transcendent and supernatural character of the kingdom of God preached by Jesus, and the central significance of the 'Son of Man,' in the revelation of the kingdom. And thereby it has re-established the conceptual connection between Jesus' and Paul's preaching. It has recognized that insofar as Paul's preaching is dominated by the idea of a redemption of both man and the world, an explanation cannot be found solely in the influence of non-Christian Hellenistic religions of redemption, but rather it must be sought in the continuation of Jesus' preaching of the coming of the kingdom.

Nevertheless, still unanswered is the essential question whether Paul's proclamation of Jesus, as the superhuman author and inaugurator of redemption, and not only its human herald, is in keeping with Jesus' self-disclosure. The consistent eschatological view remains within the radical critical tradition by giving a negative answer. Schweitzer tries to make a transition by holding that Jesus proclaimed himself to be the future bearer of redemption, *Messias designatus*, and also made a desperate unsuccessful attempt to usher in the coming of the kingdom of God. The kingdom Jesus wished did not come, and the *parousia* of the Son of Man he expected did not appear. The person of Jesus, in spite of his sacrificial death, remained on *this* side of the kingdom he had proclaimed. Bultmann does not recognize the figure of the *Messias designatus* but he agrees with Schweitzer that Jesus remained on this side of the kingdom. The main distinction between Jesus and Paul is according to Bultmann that Paul believes that with Jesus' coming and resurrection the kingdom was ushered in, whereas Jesus always spoke of the kingdom in terms of the future, and never thought of himself as the originator of the kingdom of God, but only as the preacher and herald of the kingdom.

Bultmann's conception is true to the thesis of Wrede that Paul represents another religion than Jesus. For we must concede to Wrede that the criterion of the agreement between Jesus and Paul is to be found in the position occu-

pied by the person of Jesus in their preaching: Does Jesus'
own witness to himself agree with Paul's making him to be
both the object and the subject of preaching? Is Jesus
himself the Son of Man who will come in judgment, or is he
only its herald? Is he the Son of God descended from
heaven or is he only a man, a human preacher of the word
of God which calls men to *Entscheidung*?

It is noteworthy that the newer literature rejects this
criterion as did the liberals. The question whether Jesus
actually—as recounted in the gospels—proclaimed himself
to be the Christ, the Son of God, is not considered decisive
for the heart of the Christian *kerygma* nor for the basic
agreement between Paul and Jesus. The *de-mythologizing*
(*enthmythologisierende*) interpretation of Christology, applied in another sense than that of the liberals,[1] supposedly
does not violate the *kerygma*. Although Bultmann believes
Jesus never held himself to be the Messiah, the question is
in his opinion of minor importance.[2] And on this point Bultmann's opinion carries considerable weight.[3] The gospel
is in the last analysis concerned with the recognition of Jesus
as the one whom we decisively encounter within the Word
of God. The early Christian community and Paul have
brought this recognition to expression according to the
concepts of their time in a Christological explanation. This
recognition is for us also a pure act of faith, although we are
thereby, according to Bultmann, not only independent of
the conceptions of faith of the early Christian community
and of Paul, but it is equally of no concern to us whether
Jesus considered himself to be the Messiah. Such a question
is only of historical significance and can only be answered by
the historian.[4]

Bultmann's attitude here depends on his view of the
essence of the gospel.[5] The gospel is primarily concerned
with the *Entscheidung* before which Jesus places mankind.
And this *Entscheidung*—stripped of all mythology—places

man before the question as to whether he is ready to discard the visible temporal things, over which he has control and to which, at the same time, he is bound, and to choose that over which he does not have control, the invisible; in which choice he can arrive at his existential freedom as a man. This existential choice is placed before mankind by God in a decisive manner in Jesus' preaching and cross. Bultmann believes that in his demythologizing interpretation of the *kerygma*, he can retain its essential content, its *Ereignis* (event) character, as well as the unity of the entire New Testament proclamation. For when the early Christian community, and presently also Paul, believed that Jesus was the Christ who rose from the dead, they expressed thereby their faith in the validity and *Bedeutsamkeit* (importance) of this event in a mythical manner. This confession of Jesus as the Christ is, however, not an *a priori* but an *a posteriori* confession. The faith of the church did not rest upon Jesus' messianic self-revelation and resurrection from the dead; quite the opposite is true: faith, the new *Seinsverständnis* in freedom, made Jesus to be the Messiah and led to the confession that he is the resurrected Lord.[6] The faith of the church only expressed in mythological concepts, the absolute significance of the choice confronting man in preaching and in the cross of Christ.

This is not the place to judge the demythologizing interpretation of the gospel in detail. It is based upon the anthropology of the new existentialist philosophy, and it therefore interprets the biblical opposition between sin and grace as that between the desire to be able to control what lies before one's hand, i.e., the visible world, etc., and the choice of that over which man does not have control. It reduces the gospel to the possibility of existential freedom, a possibility which man must himself realize by his *Entscheidung*. There is no place for its all-inclusive redemption of the entire cosmos at the end of this world, which finds its basis in the biblical idea of creation. There is only room for a doctrine of redemption which limits itself to spiritual freedom. And the significance ascribed to the person of Jesus is in its very basis nothing else than that of the *Preacher* and the *Example* of this *Entscheidung*. There can be no question of a forensic substitutionary atonement, and of 'the giving of one's soul as a ransom.' The absolute *Einmaligkeit* (uniqueness) of Jesus' person and work also disappears. In principle Bultmann does not get beyond the liberal view of Jesus' person and work. It is true that he opposes the liberal Jesus, as the preacher of a timeless religious moral truth, with the *Ereignis*-character of the gospel. But this *Ereignis* consists in its very depths in an appeal to *Entscheidung* which came and continues to come to man as the word of God in Jesus' preaching and self sacrifice. The Jesus of Bultmann no longer represents the idea of the Enlightenment of liberal theology. Jesus is now the one who gives modern existentialist philosophy a way of escape out of its pessimistic anthropology. However, in both instances Jesus is basically the *Preacher* and the *Example*. The question whether he considered himself to be the Christ, the natural Son of God, is irrelevant for the understanding of the kernel of the Gospel, and has nothing more than historical significance.

The situation is entirely different when one realizes that the entire New Testament *kerygma,* from the very beginning, introduces Jesus not only as the one in whom the word of God is encountered decisively by man, but above all as the one who because of his person and work has once and for all time confronted man and continues to confront him with a decision. But this decision is not to be conceived only in an anthropological existential sense, but also in a theological and cosmic sense. For the gospel is not controlled by the question as to how man can escape from his being bound to the natural and historical world and can again be brought to his own self in freedom. It is controlled by the

theological and theo-centric proclamation of the return of
the entire world, which had been corrupted by sin, to the
control of God as Creator of the heavens and the earth.[7]
Salvation is therefore connected to the person and work of
Jesus, as the Christ, in an entirely different sense than is the
case according to the conception of Bultmann. The messianic
and eschatological character of redemption is not to be
appreciated only as a mythical expression of the importance
of the existential *Entscheidung* before which Jesus places
man, but it indicates the range of the redemption sent in
him and which encompasses and includes the world and
history. Jesus is, therefore, not simply the Christ, because
man through him is brought to his own freedom, but the
opposite is the case: the freedom, the redemption, of the
gospels derives its origin and character from the messianic
and eschatological meaning of Jesus' person and work.[8]
Therefore, the question whether Jesus proclaimed himself
to be the Messiah is not only of historical significance but
it is decisive for the definition of the basic structure and the
heart of the gospel. One cannot deprive Jesus' self-revelation
of its messianic character without destroying the very Christian character of the *kerygma*. The line of demarcation
between the true and false gospel lies in the recognition of
the messianic character of Jesus' self-revelation, in the
acceptance of the official and ontical significance of his
person, as portrayed in the gospel.

In the last analysis, the question whether Jesus considered himself to be the Messiah, because of its very nature,
cannot be answered by the historian. For the New Testament *kerygma* concerning Jesus as the Messiah, and the Son
of God, rests upon his messianic self-revelation. The denial
of the latter removes the foundation of the New Testament
kerygma. To let the decision concerning Jesus' messianic
self-disclosure depend upon historical investigation means
that the actual act of faith, which the New Testament

kerygma demands, is brought under the control of historical science.[9] This state of affairs discloses how closely the faith in Jesus, as the Christ, the Son of God, is connected with the faith that the Scriptures are the authentic witness of the Holy Ghost concerning Jesus Christ (Cf. John 15:26-27). For with respect to Jesus' historical self-revelation we have no other witness than that of the Scriptures. Therefore, to recognize 'the material' authority of Jesus as the Christ, in accordance with the Christian *kerygma,* one cannot by-pass the so-called 'formal' authority of Scripture as God's witness concerning Jesus Christ.[10] The problem of "Jesus and Paul" clearly illustrates that the question: "What think ye of Christ?" despite contrary affirmations, cannot be detached from the question in which is concentrated the basis of our knowledge of the faith: "What think ye of the Scriptures?" Do they come from heaven or are they the product of man?

Nevertheless, theology must enter the historical problem concerning Jesus' messianic self-disclosure. It is not as if the treatment of the problem is able to speak the last word for our faith, but its treatment is necessary because the historical character of revelation includes historical relations which are not obvious without further examination. Therefore, the task of theology, in a thetic and anti-thetic sense is to illuminate the historical character of Jesus' messianic self-revelation and to make it as intelligible as possible. Within the cadre of our investigation before we can turn to Paul's preaching, we must pay attention to two things: the historical integrity and intelligibility of the witness of the gospels concerning Jesus' messianic self-revelation, and to the connection between Jesus' self-revelation and the faith of the early Christian community.

6. The Integrity of the Witness of the Gospels

The gospels bear uniform witness that Jesus not only thought of himself as the future *Messias designatus* or as the prophet and herald of the proximity of the kingdom of God, but Jesus also revealed himself as the present Messiah, sent by God into the world. The gospel of John may be the most explicit in its manner of expression, but the witness of the synoptic gospels is not susceptible to a different exegesis.[11] Radical criticism can ultimately not deny this fact. Bultmann, the most prominent representative of present day radical criticism, admits that the evidence of the gospel writers support the view that Jesus actually conceived of himself as being the Messiah, the Son of Man.[12] If asked what keeps him from accepting the trustworthy character of the continuous and general witness of the sources, Bultmann's answer is that Jesus' life and work, measured by the traditional ideas of the Messiah, does not display a messianic image, and nowhere within the tradition is it evident that Jesus transformed the traditional concept of the Messiah.[13] We are immediately arrested by specific elements of Jesus' self-revelation, according to the witness of the gospels. On the one hand, when Jesus speaks of the kingdom of heaven and of the Son of Man, he refers to supernatural and transcendent entities which he speaks of in terms of the future, e.g., of the future decline and renewal of the world and the future judge of the world.[14] But, on the other hand, the gospels are no less clear in their affirmation that the kingdom and the Son of Man announced by Christ was not only a future and transcendent reality, but was already a present and earthly reality. This presence was disclosed in the defeat of the devil, in Jesus' miracles, in the way in which he preached the gospel of the Kingdom, in the beatitudes with which Christ blessed the poor of spirit, a reality which finds its deepest explanation in the depths of his own person, in his power, in his being sent by God, and his being the Son of the Father. It is this two-fold unity of the future and the present, the supernatural eschatological and the human earthly, which according to the gospel witness, forms the

specific and proper content of Jesus' preaching of the kingdom and of his messianic self-revelation. Bultmann is undoubtedly correct that such a conception does not correspond
to the traditional picture of the Messiah, neither in the
national sense (the Messiah, as the 'Son of David'), nor in
the apocalyptic sense of the word (the Messiah as 'the Son
of Man'), but this fact does not prove the non-historical
character of the conception. Rather it appears from the
gospels themselves that this peculiar modality of Jesus'
messianic self-revelation instigated all sorts of questions and
tensions in John the Baptist, and in the disciples and in the
multitudes. And Jesus did not fail to answer these questions
in his reply to the question of John the Baptist (Matt.
11:2ff.), and especially in his extensive teaching to his
disciples in the parables of the kingdom (Matt. 13). In
these parables, in the very heart of the gospel, to those who
have ears to hear, Jesus intentionally speaks of this scandalous
and riddlesome modality of the coming of the kingdom and
of the Son of Man. There is here included a profound
revaluation of the current conceptions of the coming of the
kingdom and of the Son of Man; not in the sense that Jesus
eliminated the future eschatological significance of the kingdom, and of the *parousia* of the Son of Man, and reduced
the gospel to an immanent realized eschatology. Rather,
Jesus indicated how the future kingdom had already begun
in his preaching and miracles, and how the future Son of
Man is already revealed in his own person and work within
the present time. Bultmann maintains that this conception
cannot be historical because it is not clear how Jesus thought
of the relationship of his second coming, as the Son of Man,
to his earthly historical activity.[15] To those who point out
that within the gospels Jesus speaks frequently of his suffering and death as the way to his resurrection and future
glory, Bultmann replies that all such predictions could not
have originated with Jesus but must be viewed as *vaticinia*

ex eventu. To support his thesis Bultmann appeals to the undoubtedly noteworthy phenomenon[16] that in the synoptic gospels, the predictions of the *parousia* are almost never related to Jesus' suffering, death, and resurrection (Luke 17:24-25 excepted). Bultmann therefore concludes that the predictions of suffering and resurrection are secondary and originally had nothing to do with the statements of the *parousia* of the Son of Man (in which Jesus did not allude to himself).

These conceptions signify, however, a complete splitting up of the synoptic *kerygma* and the destruction of the historical picture of Jesus given in the synoptic gospels. For the predictions of the passion and the resurrection are not isolated within the gospel. They form the conclusion of a motif that from the very beginning runs through all of Jesus' words, the motif of humiliation placed upon him by the Father. His path was determined by the divine "obligation" (δει) that demanded obedience and subjection, and included humiliation and suffering. At the same time, however, he retains intact and undisturbed his consciousness of power, his self-revelation as the One who had been sent by God[17] in the absolute sense. And all this reaches its climax in the predictions of suffering and resurrection. These predictions are the completed explication of this continuous motif of humiliation and of the accompanying consciousness of being absolute. Therefore, one cannot eliminate Jesus' predictions concerning his suffering and death from the gospel as a *Fremdkörper* (alien body). By so doing one amputates and destroys the entire portrayal that the gospels— also the synoptic gospels!—give of Jesus' life on earth. It is noteworthy that Jesus' predictions concerning the *parousia* of the Son of Man mostly run parallel in the synoptic gospels with those concerning his suffering, death, and resurrection, and are not integrated into a whole. Perhaps this is an indication of the phenomenon also perceptible elsewhere in the gospels, that the full meaning of his messianic mission does not at once come to light, neither within Jesus' self-revelation, nor within the consciousness of his disciples. Undoubtedly, the prediction that the Son of Man, who is to be borne upon the clouds of heaven, and who must suffer death, signifies a complete transformation in the Jewish conception of the Messiah, and Jesus cannot directly take his disciples into his full confidence. But this does not say that the connection between the motive of suffering and the pronouncements of glorification was only brought about *ex eventu*. Rather, even though their meaning was not immediately explained in the fullest manner possible, there were within Jesus' own life two lines (which also were visible in the Old Testament): the suffering servant of the Lord, exalted by God, and the glorification of the Son of Man. This mysterious duality of being Lord and servant, of the necessity of suffering, and, nevertheless, being endowed with divine power, is the most essential element in the description all four gospels give to Jesus' earthly life.

Bultmann denies our contention with respect to the synoptic gospels, not only because he considers the predictions of suffering to be unhistorical, but also because, in his opinion, the transmitted words of Jesus do not show any trace that he was conscious of being the servant of God portrayed in Isaiah 53.[18] However, in addition to Luke 22:37 (which is again considered by Bultmann to be secondary) one can point to the peculiar influence of the language of Isaiah 53 on various statements of Jesus, which has also been noticed for example, by such authors as R. Otto,[19] G. Dalman,[20] and W. Manson.[21] Thus, for example, expressions in Mark 8:12; 8:31 and the repeated reference to the 'many,' as in Mark 10:45; 14:24. It is, however, not only a question of the words, but especially of the matter under discussion, i.e., the accent upon obedience accompanied by a consciousness of power, the readiness to accept humiliation

accompanied by the claim to exaltation. One must also point
here to Jesus' messianic self-concealment, as expressed, for
example, in his command to his disciples to keep silence.
Such a repeated phenomenon which occurs in various ways
is entirely in keeping with the historical framework of Jesus'
entry. It is the veiling of Jesus' glorification, not only *although* he is the Messiah (the Son of Man), but also *because*
he is the Messiah (the servant of the Lord).   "The Son of
Man must undergo much suffering."   In these words are
contained the mystery of Jesus' earthly concealment of his
messianic office: glorification must first be preceded by
suffering and death, and therefore the motive of disclosure
is accompanied by the motif of concealment.   In the foot-
steps of the well-known work of Wrede,[22] radical criticism
here speaks of the later 'theory of the messianic secret' in
which is to be seen the traces of the unmessianic life of the
historical Jesus. This construction, however, rests materially
on no other argument than the one mentioned, and even from
a purely historical point of view, it does not explain the
mystery of Jesus' person and work as it unmistakably appears within the gospel. Moreover, no matter what one may
think of the various parts of the tradition, Jesus derived,
on the one hand, *all his power and authority from the supernatural glory of the coming kingdom, and from the therein
expected Son of Man. And on the other hand, Jesus was conscious from the very beginning that he must in self-humiliat-
ing obedience place his life in the service of his Father. He
knew that only by giving his soul as a ransom for many
could he give the salvation of the kingdom and obtain
the glorification of the Son of Man.* These two lines of messianic glorification and messianic humiliation, which were
already traced in Old Testament prophecy, are the lines
which, according to the witness of the gospel, had determined the life of the historical Jesus and which also must

be viewed as the historical origin of the entire New Testament Christology.

7. The Origin of the Faith of the Church

All this is confirmed directly in the gospels, and later on, especially in the book of Acts, by the picture given of the origin of the faith of the disciples and the early church in Jesus as the Christ. It clearly appears that Jesus not only revealed himself to be the Messiah, but he was also recognized and professed to be such by the disciples, even though at first in a faulty manner, perhaps due to the peculiar modality of Jesus' self-disclosure. The Gospel of John discloses that this recognition already arose in the calling of the disciples, together with the influence of the preaching of John the Baptist (John 1:42ff, cf. vs. 29, 36). The synoptics also do not leave any doubt concerning this recognition, although more than in the Gospel of John, the hidden, restrained character of Jesus' self-disclosure comes to the foreground.[23] The disciples are given to understand the hiddenness of the kingdom (Matt. 13:11), which refers in the first place not simply to the content and to the meaning of the kingdom but to the fact of its presence. The modality of the presence of the kingdom is therefore made known to the disciples. And those who confessed Jesus as the Christ, the Son of the living God, also received an insight into the necessity of his suffering, death, and resurrection (Matt. 16:13ff). Thus, on the basis of the gospels, it cannot be doubted that the disciples recognized Jesus as the Messiah and that they received an incipient insight into the fulfillment he represented. This does not deny that only after the resurrection did the apostles become fully aware of the person and work of Christ. The tenor of more than one word of Jesus concerning himself then became clear. For example (Cf. John 2:22; 12:6; Luke 24:25ff), they then

were able to understand and to make known Jesus' messianic
glorification and value (Cf. Mark 4:21, 22; Matt. 10:26, 27;
17:9). They can then also in their entire preaching of Jesus
as the Christ be called witnesses of his resurrection (Acts
1:22ff). Repeatedly, we see how Jesus' messianic office is
brought into connection with his resurrection (Acts 2:36ff).
And this messiahship bears, as we shall see in more detail,
a transcendent, supernatural character. Before Jesus' death
and resurrection the disciples may have been in many ways
still in confusion and uncertainty, but his resurrection from
the dead made them know him as the supernatural Messiah,
elevated to the right hand of the Father, the Holy and Just
One (Acts 3:14; 7:52), the Prince of life (Acts 3:15), the One
proclaimed by the prophets as the Servant and Anointed
One of God (Acts 3:13, 18; Acts 4:27, 30), in short he is
described with the messianic predicates which characterize
Christ as the fulfiller of the promises, and the inaugurator
of the great final period. If one confronts 'this natural' picture of the origin and development of the faith of the early
church with the viewpoint of radical criticism, which must
explain this faith apart from Jesus' own messianic self-
disclosure and the fact of his resurrection, then the extremes
to which such reconstructions must go is evident. Such
criticism is also confronted by the fact that the early Christian community had lived from the very beginning in the
faith that Jesus was the Christ, the Son of God, in the supernatural, eschatological sense of the word. One cannot escape
asking how the early church could have derived the notion
that Jesus occupied this place in the great redemptive drama,
as the one who fulfilled the promises of God to Israel and to
the world. How could this have arisen if the church never
had noticed with respect to Jesus any messianic pretention,
and if he himself had never claimed such an absolute, divine
significance for his own person?

It is thought that the early Christian community, after

what has been called its 'resurrection experience,' applied to
Jesus existing religious conceptions of the Messiah, or conceptions of a super-human being derived from other religions. However, it must be realized that nearly every word
in this reconstruction of history implies a new problem. Undoubtedly, one cannot proceed without ascribing great significance to the resurrection faith. Nevertheless, the same
question remains: What is the basis of this faith? Does it
rest upon the fact of the resurrection as described in the
gospels? In this case there is no reason to doubt the historicity of Jesus' messianic self-revelation. For Jesus' resurrection from the dead is the most authentic and undeniable
confirmation of his messianic self-disclosure. Radical criticism, however, will no more hear of the factuality of Jesus'
resurrection from the dead, than of his messianic witness to
himself. The possibility of basing the faith of the early
Christian community upon the experience of the resurrection
is, therefore, not open to radical criticism. For the latter must
first explain the origin of this 'experience' of the resurrection.
One is here involved in a vicious circle by trying to solve one
riddle by means of another. On the one hand, the attempt is
made to explain the faith that Jesus is the supernatural, eschatological Son of Man in terms of the resurrection experience.
On the other hand, to make this resurrection experience—
without resurrection—historically acceptable in any sense,
one must fall back upon the tremendous impression which
Jesus' eschatological *Entscheidungsruf* (call to decision)
made upon his disciples, by which they could then understand Jesus as the one in whose person God accomplished
the great decision, i.e., as the Son of Man. It is clear that
to explain the faith of the church radical criticism must also
fall back upon the mystery which lurked in Jesus himself.
Radical criticism refuses to recognize in Jesus himself the
claim to be the Messiah, the Son of Man, who through his
suffering and death was to be glorified by God the Father.

Instead it believes that such notions were in fact ascribed
to Jesus by the creative, mythologizing faith of the church.
On this standpoint it is completely incomprehensible how
the apostles who supposedly never heard Jesus' own claim
to be the Messiah, and in spite of his crucifixion, which was
to them unintelligible, nevertheless, directly after his death
confessed him to be the Messiah and the Son of Man, resurrected by God from the dead. It is said that every period
has its own "theological explication of the redemptive events
and of Christian existence."[24] But what is not explained is,
how the disciples could have conceived of Jesus' death as a
redemptive event and of their own situation as 'Christian
existence'; in other words, in what way could the unmessianic
preaching, the unmessianic life and the unmessianic death of
the historical Jesus, from which a compelling force proceeded
to an *Entscheidung* (decision), lead directly after his death
to a faith in his messianic resurrection. One cannot appeal
here to the 'theological explication' of the time in question,
for it is just here in this crucial and decisive point that the
religionsgeschichtliche explanation fails completely. For
neither contemporary Judaism or Greek conceptions can
offer help or furnish any light. The Jewish conception is of
no help because the figure of the suffering, dying, and resurrected Messiah was entirely strange,[25] both to the earthly
national expectation of the Messiah, and also to the eschatological apocalyptic conceptions of the Son of Man. Greek
thought is even less suitable, for even if one can point to the
idea of 'dying and rising gods,' it is clear that the origin
of the faith of the early Christian community cannot be thus
explained. All affirmations (as in Gunkel) of the intrusion
of alien religious motives into the church, directly after Jesus'
death, cannot change the undeniable fact that the faith of
the church, that Jesus was resurrected from the dead, did not
rest upon a syncretism but upon other realities, which cannot be explained in terms of the history or the psychology of

religion in any single respect.[26] An historical riddle confronts anyone unwilling to seek these realities within Jesus' messianic self-disclosure and in his factual resurrection from the dead. The early Christian community is then held responsible for a Christology, the foundations of which have been destroyed. A miracle is removed and a riddle is introduced in its stead; the historicity of the messianic office and the resurrection of Jesus is denied, to be replaced by the inexplicable, mythical figure of the Christ of the early Christian church. It is clear that in all this something else is at stake other than the results of historical critical investigation. It seems rather that history and criticism must first be silenced in order to be able to elude the faith in the factuality of Jesus' supernatural, eschatological messiahship.

On the other hand, it is observed from the little developed Christology of the Book of Acts, that faith in Jesus as the Christ only came to the fore after his death, and thus could not have rested upon his own witness to himself. One speaks in this connection of the adoptionism of Acts, and it is thought that whereas Jesus, according to the conception of the Christian church of Jerusalem, was viewed before his death and resurrection only as a man among men, as a prophet and servant of God, after his resurrection from the dead, he was made by God to be the Lord and Christ. According to this conception it appears from the book of Acts that faith in Jesus as the Messiah was the fruit of the faith in his resurrection.[27]

To judge this view one must first consider such passages as Acts 2:36; 3:13; 13:33, in which Jesus' glorification and messianic legitimacy is repeatedly related to his resurrection; Acts 2:36 is here especially of importance. "Therefore let all the house of Israel know assuredly, that God hath made that same Jesus whom ye have crucified, both the Lord and Christ." It appears to follow that before Jesus' resurrection these predicates were not applicable to Jesus,

and that God by raising Jesus from the dead only then had
adopted him as his Messiah. It has been correctly observed,
however, that such an adoptionism cannot be derived from
the statement that Jesus was made to be Lord by his
exaltation. In the same manner, in Philippians 2:5ff, it is
said of him who became obedient unto death, even the death
of the cross, that God hath given him the name 'Lord,' while,
at the same time, Philippians 2:5ff, testifies with the greatest
emphasis to the pre-existent glory of Christ.[28] There is then
also no reason to base this theory of adoptionism on the
expression 'to be made Christ.'[29] According to the analogy
of the words 'to be made to be the Lord,' one can explain
the expression 'to be made Christ,' as simply being endowed
with messianic glory and power[30] (Cf. Matt. 28:18). And
what is revelant to Acts 2:36 can also be applied to Acts
13:33, where the messianic utterance of Psalm 2, "Thou art
my Son; Today I have chosen thee," is applied to the resurrection of Jesus from the dead. Also here one does not need
to think of an adoption *theologoumenon* either on the part
of the writer of Acts, or in terms of a *vorlukanischen Zeit*
(pre-Lukan period), to which Luke might have returned.[31]
Sevenster correctly points to Romans 1:3, 4, where it is also
said that Christ, by his resurrection from the dead, is de-
clared to be the Son of God in power, and where there
cannot be any question of an adoptionistic conception.[32]
When Psalms 2:7 is applied, as we believe it to be,[33] to the
resurrection, this is not to be understood in an exclusive, but
in an inclusive sense. The fact that Jesus by the resurrection
is made to participate in the messianic glory does not need
to exclude the fact that he already was the Messiah, in the
proper sense of the word. Such passages as Acts 2:22;
17:31, where Jesus is called 'a man,' or in 3:22, where he is
called 'a prophet,' do not give any reason to think of a period
in which Jesus was only viewed as a man. To understand
such a qualification, not in the sense of adoptionism but as

a gradual missionary approach,[34] one must rather consider the circumstances under which (according to Luke) these terms were used (the very first preaching to the Jews, and Paul's address on the Areopagus).

Such passages as these, viewed in themselves, offer no basis for such an adoptionistic Christology within the book of Acts, nor within the early Christian church at Jerusalem. Such a conception is still less acceptable when in the second place one remembers that Acts is a sequel to the gospel of Luke within which, even as within the other gospels, Jesus' supernatural, messianic authenticity and glory already constitute the great content of his earthly life.[35] It is, therefore, obvious that the writer of Acts (which is not a dogmatic historical treatise on the faith of the first Christian church, but in which the preaching of Christ is continued) did not intend in his second book to propagate a Christological view which deviated from his first gospel account. To be able to find this adoptionistic Christology within Acts one must presuppose that an adoptionistic Christology was already present within certain old formulations, in spite of and apart from the consciousness of the author.[36] At the same time one must assume that the Christology of the author's gospel account (that was written before that of Acts, and according to his own words was intended to be only an accurate, written record of what he had seen as an eye witness and of what had been delivered to him, Luke 1:1-4) represents a later development in the faith of the early Christian Church. Even though the *formgeschichtliche* interpretation of Acts and of the gospels does not hesitate to accept these conclusions, such an hypothesis must, nevertheless, even on the basis of general historical considerations, be considered extremely precarious. In the first place it denies to the writer of the gospel and of Acts the necessary power to distinguish such an important point as the faith in Jesus as the Christ. But it also presupposes in the generation for whom Luke writes his gospel (i.e., the generation of those who had known and heard the eye witnesses and to some extent had themselves been eye witnesses) a complete lack of knowledge concerning Jesus' self-revelation during his sojourn on earth. Presumably this generation permitted itself to be told by Luke and the other evangelists that during his earthly life Jesus had already revealed himself to be the Christ sent by God, whereas in reality the 'experience of the resurrection' actually lay at the foundation of every 'explicit' Christology. And, in support of this far-reaching affirmation, there is no other evidence than a few adoptionistic formulations of which the author himself was unaware, in his *own* second book!

Naturally, we have not affirmed that the early Christian church of Jerusalem, or even the apostles, had or could have had from the very beginning a complete and final Christology. Nor do we deny that the resurrection of Christ was an event of decisive and great significance for their faith and insight into the person and work of Jesus. We are rather extremely conscious of how unspeakably difficult it is for us to form a clear historical picture of the origin of the faith in Jesus' messiahship and of its implications. It is again evident that the kerygmatic character also of the historical books of the New Testament is accompanied by a certain incompleteness with respect to secondary historical questions. One thing is, however, to be deduced from the preceding: to do justice to the position which the person of Jesus as the Christ assumes within Paul's preaching, one cannot by-pass the early Christian church. And to understand the faith of the early Christian church without accepting the factuality of Jesus' messianic self-disclosure and resurrection, brings with it unsolvable historical riddles. The relevance of our discussion thus far to our theme will be more in evidence when we now turn to Paul's preaching of Jesus as the Christ.

CHAPTER III

THE SOURCES OF PAUL'S PREACHING

8. *Knowledge of Jesus "According to the Flesh"*

Before treating the actual content of Paul's preaching it is important to examine what he himself states to be its sources. In this respect Paul cannot be placed on the same level with the other apostles who, according to the words of Peter, were the witnesses, "of all things which he did both in the land of the Jews and in Jerusalem; whom they slew and hanged on a tree; him God raised up the third day and shewed him openly; not to all the people but unto witnesses chosen before of God, even to us, who did eat and drink with him after he rose from the dead. And he commanded us to preach unto the people and to testify that it is he who was ordained of God to be the Judge of quick and dead" (Acts 10:39:42). In this sense Paul cannot be called a witness of Jesus. What then were the sources which Paul had at hand for his lofty proclamation of Jesus as the Christ? And for such an investigation there exists all the more reason, because with respect to the origins of Paul's Christology it is thought that all sorts of alien non-Christian influences can be indicated.

The first question to be dealt with is whether one can assume with good ground that Paul knew Jesus during his public ministry in Galilee or during the course of his suffering. Especially, liberal theology, which wishes to explain Paul's Christology in terms of the loftiness of Jesus' *moral personality* has accepted or posited the notion that Paul knew

Jesus.[1] One passage in the epistles is relevant in support
of Paul's personal knowledge of the incarnate Christ. In
2 Corinthians 5:16, Paul writes: "Yea though we have known
Christ after the flesh, yet now henceforth know we him no
more."[2] Even though many take this verse to indicate that
Paul knew Christ personally, we believe that such a conclusion cannot be drawn from this passage. Paul probably
had his opponents in mind here, when he was discussing the
question of the knowledge of Christ 'according to the flesh'
(the relationship to Jesus when he still was on earth). Those
who may consider such a knowledge indispensable for
preaching must remember that the preaching of Christ and
faith in Christ is now no longer dependent upon the knowledge of Christ according to the flesh. For consider once—
one must here paraphrase—that someone, whether myself
or another, had known Christ in this manner, such a relationship now no longer exists, because Christ is dead and the
believers owe their lives only to the dead and resurrected
Christ, and must therefore also be directed to him.[3] Paul
does not here say, therefore, that he has known Jesus according to the flesh. A positive conclusion cannot be drawn
here. It would seem that a negative conclusion would be
more in keeping with the passage, because if Paul had known
Jesus in all probability he would not have spoken of it in
such a purely hypothetical manner.[4] No matter what the
truth of the matter may be, it is clearly evident in any case
that Paul does not reduce what he knows of Jesus here or
elsewhere to his personal acquaintance with Jesus during the
latter's life on earth. It will subsequently appear[5] that in
opposition to the previously mentioned liberal conception,
the *religionsgeschichtliche* school, in support of its own mystical pneumatic conception of Pauline Christology,[6] has incorrectly drawn the conclusion that Paul breaks every relation
with the historical Christ in order to appeal for his knowledge
of Christ solely to his communion with the risen Lord. From

2 Corinthians 5:16, one can in any case find no support for
the opinion that Paul came under the control of Jesus' 'moral
personality' by his personal contact with Jesus.

The question on what does Paul base his preaching of
Jesus as the Christ is answered by Paul's epistles and the
book of Acts. This answer is twofold: first, on the *revelation*
which he personally experienced, and second, on the *tradition*
known already to the established church.

9. Revelation

Concerning the first point, Paul appeals for his knowledge of Christ more than once to the revelation which he
had experienced at *his conversion.* He speaks of this in
1 Corinthians 15:8: "and last of all he was seen of me also
as of one born out of due time,"[7] and he places this on the
same level as the appearance[8] of Christ to Cephas, to the
twelve, and to the five hundred brethren. The appearance
of Christ to the apostles must not be valued as only personal
experience, but especially as the foundation of preaching
(the witness of the resurrection) and for the gathering of
the church. Likewise, Paul's knowledge of Jesus as the
Christ, and his apostolic calling must also be based upon
this appearance of the resurrected Lord.[9] To prove the
legitimacy of his apostolic office Paul appeals to the 'seeing'
of the Lord, conceived of in this sense (1 Cor. 9:1; 2 Cor.
4:6). In Galatians 1 and 2, which is so important for our
knowledge of Paul's calling, he speaks of the appearance
of Christ as *God's revelation of* his Son in me that I might
preach him among the heathen (Gal. 1:16).[10] It appears
here clearer than anywhere else that Paul owed his knowledge of Christ as the Son of God to this revelation.[11] Also
the fact that God himself is mentioned as the subject of
revelation is of importance. God revealed to him his Son
so that he might *preach him among the heathen.'* In this

revelation Paul is not only converted but he received, through the God who set him apart from his mother's womb and called him by his grace (Gal. 1:15), the true knowledge of Christ, which he needed for his preaching of the gospel (Cf. also 2 Cor. 4:6).[12]

The significance of Paul's conversion can thus be viewed in the correct light. The attempt has been made to approach[13] Paul's conversion from the standpoint of the psychology of religion, and then to make it the basis of the contrast in Paul's preaching between the life of faith and the life of the works of the law. His conversion thus signifies a breaking through of a previously developed religious process, an inner conflict that affected his religious certainty, and which can be more exactly characterized as a polar opposition between faith and works, freedom and slavery, letter and spirit, and such concepts are understood in whatever way Paul's preaching is conceived of in general. The older (and present) orthodox theology, as far as it supports this conception, maintains to the fullest degree, the supernatural character of the emancipation of Paul's soul (often compared to Luther's conversion). However, since the Tübingen school, the attempt has been made to understand this conversion in a rational psychological manner.[14] In both instances, however, Paul's conversion is viewed as a solution to an inner crisis,[15] in which Paul found himself in an increasing degree, and which came to a solution and focal point on the road to Damascus. But the sources offer no evidence of such a process of conversion and of such a negative preparation for Paul's later gospel proclamation. One can undoubtedly say that the death of the Messiah, as proclaimed by the disciples of Jesus, must have signified a question for Paul.[16] But that this death also *actually* operated in Paul in such a way that it shocked his feeling of certainty, and even caused him to question whether he was on the right path, is in our opinion not to be derived from any single datum.

In opposition to our point of view some believe they can find support for their position in Acts 26:14: "It is hard for thee to kick against the pricks." It is thought that it can be deduced from this that Paul already before his conversion was touched within his conscience, and tried to smother this voice by terrible persecution.[17] It is correctly pointed out by others, however, that this idea, even though it includes certain possibilities, does not rest upon established data.[18] Even if one understands by the 'pricks' certain specific voices which came to him before his conversion, and against which he struggled, it does not follow that he was disturbed by them and his conscience was troubled by them.[19] But the conception that 'the kicking against the pricks' refers to Paul's opposition to voices of conscience, which came to him before his conversion, goes too far in a psychological direction, and reads more into the text than is actually to be found. The expression is simply an indication of the fruitlessness of Paul's terrible persecution of Jesus and his church. The entire expression points to the supremacy of the risen Lord, not to the situation of Paul's conscience before or after his conversion.[20] Not only must every rational psychological explanation of Paul's conversion[21] be abandoned but the meaning of his conversion must not be sought in the subjective, soteriological sphere but in the objective, Christological sphere. That Jesus of Nazareth, who was crucified by the Jews, and persecuted by Paul in his church, was exalted into the heavens and clothed with the divine power of the Son of God, was the tremendous certainty which grasped Paul upon the road to Damascus, and which formed the starting point and the great content of his gospel proclamation. Such is evident not only from Galatians 1:16[22] but also from such passages as 2 Corinthians 4:6; Timothy 1:13, in which we acquire the unmistakable impression that this revelation occurred against all expectation and inclination of his conscience, while he was in the state of full conviction, unbelief, and ignorance, and while, without his conscience in any way being aroused, he wished to eradicate the name of Jesus of Nazareth and to persecute his church. And our position is confirmed by the book of Acts in its threefold picture of his conversion, which lays the emphasis upon the unexpected and overwhelming character of the conversion, and which at the first was entirely incomprehensible to Paul (Acts 9:3-5; 22:6-8; 26:15). While convinced it was his duty to fight against the name of Jesus with all severity (Acts 26:9), he was suddenly confronted with Jesus the Nazarene, whom he previously knew as an historical person, who then appeared in the heavens in his divine glory. *In this encounter with the person of the exalted Christ is to be found the starting point of Paul's apostolic preaching, as well as the real significance of his conversion, and it is this confrontation to which he appeals again and again to justify his preaching of Christ.*[23]

10. Tradition

In the light of the available historical data one must lay all emphasis upon the fundamental significance of the appearance of Christ to Paul, as the source and content of his apostolic proclamation of Christ. However, in the second place, this must not close our eyes to the great importance that the *tradition* of the early Christian church had for his preaching. This importance is misunderstood by many, especially by those who see an unbridgeable cleft between 'the historical Jesus,' and the Christ of Paul. It is generally thought that although Paul's conversion (no matter how it is conceived of) had wrought a decisive change in his view of Jesus of Nazareth, it did not cause him to ascribe special significance to the historical picture of Jesus as retained, for

example, within the synoptic tradition (with the exception
of Jesus' death and resurrection). And this is thought to
have directed Paul's attention entirely to the pneumatic
knowledge of the heavenly Christ.[24] In opposition to our
thesis, which would do justice to the dependence of Paul
upon the apostolic tradition concerning Jesus' temporal
earthly life, a plea is apparently made to Paul's own statements in Galatians 1, that he did not receive his gospel from
man, but through the revelation of Jesus Christ, Galatians
1:12, and that after his conversion he did not consult with
flesh or blood ("neither went I up to Jerusalem to them which
were apostles before me, but I went into Arabia, and returned again to Damascus. Then after three years I went
up to Jerusalem to see Peter," Gal. 1:18ff). To such passages
an appeal is made again and again by those who would
view Paul's preaching of Christ as something essentially new,
as something entirely different from the message of Jesus
himself, and who would deny, if not his knowledge, at least
his interest in the historical life of Jesus.[25]

Undoubtedly Galatians 1:12ff contains strong proof,
not only of the independence of Paul's position with respect
to the admission of the pagan world, but also for the independence of his proclamation of Christ, since it is not determined by the teaching of the apostles. What happened to
Paul at Damascus provisionally at least made any further
preparation for his apostolic office superfluous. But it does
not follow, however, that Paul's proclamation of the gospel
was detached from that of the apostles of Jerusalem. It
does not follow that his confession of and preaching of Jesus
as the Christ had its own content, which differed from that
of the apostles, or that he had no interest in the tradition of
the eye witnesses, concerning that which was taught by
Jesus and which occurred with respect to him. Rather, on
good grounds the opposite must be accepted.

a. First one may not separate the statements in Galatians

1:11-12 from their context and purpose. Paul would defend
himself against the accusation that his gospel bore an entirely
secondary and derivative character, because he did not
belong to the original company of the apostles. It has therefore been said correctly that on the basis of these verses one
should not make Paul into a theological New Testament
Melchizedek, without father, mother, or genealogy, and that
under other circumstances, he would gladly have acknowl-
edged what he owed to the original apostles.[26]

b. Secondly, in spite of all arguments to the contrary,[27]
before his conversion Paul had intercourse with Jerusalem
and there came into direct contact with the original church.
This is firmly established on the basis of the repeated and
unanimous witness of Acts (Cf. 7:58; 8:1, 3; 9:1, 13, 21; 22:3ff;
26:4ff, 10). There is also nothing in his epistles in conflict
with this, not even Galatians 1:22, to which an appeal is
frequently made.[28] For that Paul lived in Jerusalem as a
young man, and received instructions in the law from
Gamaliel (Acts 9:1), and that he went to persecute the
church, with the mandate of the Jewish authorities, does
not in any way need to exclude the fact that he was *personally*
($\tau\hat{\omega}$ $\pi\rho\sigma\omega\pi\omega$) unknown to the churches of Judea (apparently
Jerusalem is not primarily thought of here). Paul, in verse
23, apparently would not deny that they knew him and had
heard of him (they had heard "that he who had formerly
persecuted us, now proclaims the faith"). Therefore, it is
entirely inadequate, on the basis of Galatians 1:22, to deny
Paul's past in Jerusalem, which is again and again mentioned in the book of Acts, and to make Paul into a purely
diaspora Jew, and to make this scepticism responsible for
the construction of a Hellenistic primal Christianity, and a
dominating Hellenistic interpretation of Paul's theology.[29]
Rather Paul's spiritual origin in Palestinian Judaism is established by Paul himself in such passages as Philippians 3:5;
2 Corinthians 11:22.[30]

To what extent Paul was informed of that which was
experienced in the first Christian community before his conversion, cannot be established in detail because the sources
are silent. There can be no doubt, however, concerning the
fact that Paul knew that the early church of Jerusalem believed in Jesus as the Christ. This preaching of Jesus of
Nazareth, as the crucified and risen Messiah, was that which
was proclaimed by the apostles from the very beginning
(Acts 2, 3), and was that which aroused the hostility of the
Jews (Acts 4:10,17; Acts 5:28-31, 40, 42; 7:56, 57), and that
against which Paul also directed his attack (Acts 26:9).

Moreover, it appears from Acts 7:58, Acts 8:1ff, that
Paul was a witness to the death of Stephen, and in fact to a
certain degree he also took part in his execution, or in any
case approved it. From this fact one may conclude that
Paul was well informed of what was proclaimed by Stephen,
and since he himself originated out of the *Diaspora*, it is very
possible that he had united with the Synagogue of foreign
Jews in Jerusalem (Acts 6:9), to which belonged the most
rabid opponents of Stephen. Of the latter we are told that
they debated with Stephen; perhaps one can even dare to
presuppose[31] that Paul took part and thereby acquired more
exact knowledge of the faith of the early church with
respect to the person and the work of Jesus. In any case it is
evident how closely Paul was related to the first conflicts at
Jerusalem between the followers and the opponents of Jesus.

From all this it follows clearly that the revelation given
to Paul gave him the correct view of the faith of the church
at Jerusalem. It was not only a revelation of the heavenly
Jesus, but also the proof that the persecuted faith in Jesus
as the Christ, and the faith in the entrance of the messianic
redemptive period was the true faith. We read also that
Paul after his conversion immediately proclaimed that Jesus
is the Son of God (Acts 9:20), and confused the Jews in
Damascus by "affirming that this was the Christ." Even

though this preaching in a certain sense rested solely upon revelation it was not thinkable without a connection with that which occurred at Jersualem, and thus unthinkable without a previous tradition.

c. That Paul, if not immediately, was later informed of a detailed tradition concerning the life, death, and resurrection of Christ, is proven by his letters. Undoubtedly, the reproduction of Jesus' words form only a small part of the content of Paul's epistles. The central point of Paul's proclamation of Christ is formed much more by what occurred to Jesus, especially the cross and resurrection, than by that which was said and done by him. However, this does not imply that Paul was ignorant of Jesus' preaching and life, nor does it remove the fact that he shows himself to be dependent upon tradition for the more exact knowledge of Jesus' death and resurrection. One thinks especially of such words as 1 Thessalonians 4:15ff, where for the sequence of the events at the return of Christ, Paul appeals to 'a word of the Lord.' Likewise, he distinguishes in 1 Corinthians 7 between Jesus' words concerning the marriage state and his own (Cf. 10, 12, 25, 40). Also the rule that those who proclaim the gospel shall live by the gospel is called by him an ordinance of the Lord (1 Cor. 9:14). Of special importance in this connection is the recitation of the institution of the Lord's supper in 1 Corinthians 11:23-25, where the *termini technici*[32] for the receiving and transmission of tradition are used by Paul,[33] and the description in Corinthians 15:1, 3 of the gospel in general, and of the message of Jesus' death, burial, and resurrection, in particular, with the same words (παραλαμβάνω and παραδίδωμι).

In addition there are still a number of expressions which can be cited which do not expressly speak of a 'word' or 'tradition' of the Lord, but where such words clearly lay at the foundation of Paul's exhortation as, for example, in Romans 12:14 ("bless them who persecute you"); 13:9 (Cf.

Gal. 5:14, the summary of the law); 1 Corinthians 13:2 ("the faith that moves mountains"), and others.[34]

It ought to be remembered that Paul's epistles do not contain basic missionary preaching but they are occasional writings directed to churches and people who have already come to the Christian faith and for whom the first instruction concerning Jesus, his person, teaching, and work did not need to be repeated. Only in such instances where it was necessary does Paul repeat the historical tradition; thus, for example, in addition to the institution of the Lord's supper he repeats the tradition concerning the resurrection of Christ. From this it also appears that Paul is not indifferent or ignorant of the historical, but that he goes into details and appeals to the tradition as he had received and proclaimed it in his basic missionary preaching to the church. Of special importance here is 1 Corinthians 15:1ff: "Moreover brethren I declare unto you the gospel which I preached unto you, which also ye have received, and wherein ye stand"; and then follows: "For I delivered unto you first of all that which I also received, how that Christ died for our sins according to the Scriptures," etc. It is true that the central point of Paul's preaching is not that of Jesus' preaching, but is rather his person, in his humiliation and exaltation. And within the center of Paul's preaching there is reflected the eradicable impression of the appearance of Jesus on the road to Damascus. However, this does not in any way imply that the tradition concerning Jesus' earthly life and work was of little importance to Paul. One cannot expect anything else from an apostle who had Barnabas, Silas, John, Mark and Luke as his fellow-workers, and from an apostle who proclaimed Jesus Christ as an historical person to the pagan world. Again and again even in the most exalted Christological statements such as Philippians 2:6-8, Romans 15:3, 2 Corinthians 8:9, Galatians 4:4, there clearly comes to the fore the historical picture of Jesus in his earthly wanderings

and humiliation, a knowledge of the tradition concerning
Jesus, appears as one of the essential presuppositions of
Paul's gospel proclamation.[35]

d. Of special significance for an insight into Paul's
attitude with respect to tradition and thereby also for the
entire problem of Jesus and Paul is provided in the last
analysis by the fact that in the entire New Testament there
is no discrepancy or conflict between Paul and the early
Christian church at Jerusalem, and its leaders (the apostles)
with respect to the proclamation of Jesus Christ. The very
opposite is the case. Not only does Paul testify expressly
that three years after his conversion he had fellowship for
a period with Peter, in which time he had the opportunity
to become better acquainted with the apostolic preaching.[36]
But, insofar as there were any differences of opinion these
concerned the application of the doctrine of redemption to
the pagan world (Gal. 2, Acts 15), but never the person
and work of Jesus Christ. When one remembers that the
apostles were eye witnesses and that Paul was called to be
an apostle only a short time after Jesus' death, it is historically
unthinkable that Paul could have proclaimed a different
gospel concerning Christ without getting into difficulty with
'Jerusalem.' This historical circumstance is, without even
considering all the arguments derived from the proclamation
itself, one of the most powerful counter arguments against
the opinion that Paul introduced an entirely new proclamation of Jesus as the Christ, and was even the second originator
of Christianity.

Anyone who thoughtfully reads the epistles of Paul
notices that there is never any indication of a difference with
the apostles or the early church concerning the content of
the gospel. Paul recognizes only one gospel and when another message is called the gospel, this is nothing else than
a misuse of the word, met by Paul with irony and serious
condemnation (Gal. 1:6ff; 1 Cor. 16:22; 2 Cor. 11:3, 4).

Only a single foundation can be laid. Whether or not this
has been laid by Paul or by another is immaterial (1 Cor.
3:5ff).[37] That Paul recognizes himself to be entirely in
agreement with the other apostles appears from 1 Corinthians 15:3ff; Galatians 2:15ff. Nowhere does he contend
that the other apostles proclaim anything different (Cf. 1 Cor.
9:14).

Whoever believes there is a cleft between Jesus' and
Paul's gospel must also accept the same cleft between Jesus
and the early church. This argument that was advanced by
Schweitzer[38] from the very beginning against the *religionsgeschichtliche* explanation of Paul in terms of the Hellenistic
religiosity correctly continues to play a great role[39] in the
problem of Jesus and Paul. Machen correctly writes: "The
really astounding fact, which emerges from all discussion
of the apostolic age, is that the Pauline conception of the
person of Christ, whatever may be said of the Pauline doctrine of Gentile freedom, was never criticized by the original
apostles. Indeed, so far as can be seen, it was never criticized
even by the Judaizers themselves. Apparently it never occurred to Paul that his conception of the heavenly Christ
required defense. About other things there was controversy;
the doctrine of Christian freedom, for example, had to be
defended against all sorts of objections and by the use of all
sorts of evidence. But about the person of Christ there was
not one word of debate."[40] And elsewhere, "the fact is of
enormous importance. The heavenly Christ of Paul was also
the Christ of those who had walked and talked with Jesus
of Nazareth."[41]

11. Paul's Relationship to the Pagan World

The question is what other sources in addition to the
ones mentioned could have been employed by Paul or
actually were employed by him in his preaching of Christ.

The *religionsgeschichtliche* school is, as we have frequently noticed, of the opinion that Paul, especially in Christological conceptions, was deeply influenced by Hellenistic
heathendom, and probably also by non-canonical Jewish
writings and ideas. In pursuing our study we shall have to
go into the material significance of this conception in greater
detail. But in this connection we must emphasize two things.

In the first place a distinction ought to be made between
Hellenistic influences in Paul, and the accusation that he
mixed the gospel of Jesus Christ with pagan and syncretistic
articles of faith.

That in spite of his Jewish origin and education, Paul
must have had the opportunity of acquiring a knowledge
of pagan life, culture, and religion is directly evident when
one remembers he was from Tarsus (Acts 21:39; 22:3), and
his long sojourn there after his conversion (Acts 9:30; 11:25),
and when one also takes into account what the book of
Acts states of Paul's journeys to Asia and Europe, and his
fellowship with all levels of the population (Acts 13:7ff;
13:44; 14:1; 17:5, 12), and his oration at the Areopagus at
Athens (Acts 17:18ff), and his appearance in a pagan school
at Ephesus (Acts 19:9).[42] That such a man as Paul actually
acquired this knowledge, and would seriously assimilate
in his language, appearance, manners and method of teaching that which would assist him in making a good impression on those to whom he directs himself is not only a
general conclusion to be drawn, but one which can be derived from the picture given in both Acts and in his own
epistles (compare for example Acts 17:22ff, 28; 1 Cor.
9:21-23; 10:24-28, 33; 15:33; Titus 1:12). The extent to
which Paul wishes to open the door to the pagans is evident especially from the hard struggle which he had to free
them from the ceremonial law, and from his censure
even of Peter and Barnabas, who in principle were in agreement with Paul, but were not yet conscious of the con-

sequence of their own principles (Gal. 2:11ff). All this indicates how much Paul, in principle and in practice was in-
clined to approach the pagans with the gospel in their own
style of living and social forms, even though it is not easy
to indicate this in all its detail and concreteness.[43] This is
especially true of the question to what degree Paul employed
the terminology of the pagan outlook and religion in order
to translate the gospel into terms intelligible to *heathendom*
while at the same time proclaiming it in opposition to pagan
religions. As long as the connection is considered to be
simply formal (if it is not judged by too narrow standards)
it fits within the cadre of Paul's actions and life's work.
However, one must directly add that those who lay such
a strong emphasis on such a formal connection usually find
here a point of entry for all sorts of pagan conceptions within
the Christian proclamation.[44] This brings us to the question
of a religious syncretism.

In this respect, one ought in the *second* place, to
establish, as a matter of basic importance for the insight into
Paul's preaching, the fact that Paul himself, in the writings
which we have in our possession, never laid any positive
connection between the gospel of Jesus Christ and the
pagan world of his day, and that everything which the
religionsgeschichtliche school refers to as a syncretism in Paul
rests upon conclusions unsupported by Paul's attitude to
heathendom. Even stronger: whereas, in the case of various
pagan religions and cults in Paul's day, there exists a great
degree of mutual toleration,[45] Paul's preaching of Jesus
Christ is as exclusive (1 Cor. 8:5-6), and his rejection of
the pagan polytheism and conceptions of God, is as absolute
as possible. And in opposition he posits his own gospel,
which is an offense to the Jews and foolishness to Greeks
(1 Cor. 1:21; 8:4; 10:19; Gal. 4:8; 1 Thess. 4:5; 2 Thess.
1:8). Also when Paul admits a pagan knowledge of God
and God's revelation, at least in the letters we have, this

does not serve as a rational introduction to be laid at the foundation of his preaching, or as a structure the heathen already possess in their own way, on which he can build. Rather, he speaks of their knowledge of God to accuse them of suppressing all true knowledge of God, and as the motive prompting the revelation of the wrath of God against them (Rom. 1:18ff).[46] This does not mean that Paul did not attach any positive importance for the proclamation of the gospel[47] to the pagan consciousness of God, and to their desire for salvation, which in spite of their pagan and false religions continued to be in evidence. Nevertheless, the nature of the gospel of Christ and the conception of the way of salvation which it contains is opposed again and again by Paul in an absolute antithesis to that which was current among the pagans (1 Cor. 1:20ff; 2:6; 3:18ff; 2 Cor. 4:4; here also Acts 17:32). The endeavor as, for example, in the various phases of the *religionsgeschichtliche* school to make Paul's preaching, especially his Christological statements in which the antithesis takes on its sharpest form, dependent upon the pagan world, is then completely in conflict with the deepest motives of Paul's preaching among the pagans.

12. The Significance of the Pneuma

Especially with respect to Paul's preaching of Christ it has been held that Paul's own statements disclose that the knowledge he claimed to have of Christ, if not in content, at least with regard to its sources, displays a striking agreement with the pagan gnosticism of his day. We must now return to the opinion that Paul considered the knowledge of the historical Jesus—what we have described as the *tradition*—to be of little or no significance, and that for his own preaching and views of Christ, he trusted exclusively to that which he was given by the *pneuma*. Paul's preaching of Christ ought, therefore, not to be described as historical but as pneumatic. Within his own preaching, Paul appears as a full-fledged gnostic,[48] and such words as *'gnosis,' 'mysterion,' 'sophia'* when used to describe the heart of the gospel ought to be understood in this light. In addition to the passages to which we have already referred to, Galatians 1:16ff,[49] and 2 Corinthians 5:16, an appeal in support of this opinion is made to the well-known *"pneuma-passage"* (1 Cor. 2:6-16),[50] in which Paul speaks of the hidden wisdom of God as a mystery which God reveals by the Spirit to the spiritual man. And to this can then be added all passages where Paul speaks of the gospel of Christ as a mystery, which God has now revealed (Rom. 16:25-26, etc.).

Now we cannot here treat the difficult question as to how far Paul, especially in his letter to the Corinthians (in connection with their 'spiritual' knowledge) makes use of the terminology of the mysteries of the gnosis.[51] The question which now occupies us and is of actual importance is: for his knowledge and faith in Christ, to what extent does Paul appeal to such an internal (understood in a gnostic sense) revelation of the Holy Spirit, and to what degree does he make it the source of his preaching of Christ?

The general answer is that any attempt to find an opposition in Paul between the pneumatic and historical (traditional) knowledge of Jesus Christ is in conflict with the most characteristic element of Paul's preaching. Paul's Christology is not timeless and inward, but the historical and objective aspects of Christ's coming into the world, his suffering, death, and resurrection constitutes its very essence. Therefore, apart from the question whether Paul employed the terminology of the mysteries[52] (in addressing the Corinthians) the expression 'the hidden wisdom of God,' which God reveals by the Spirit to 'them that are perfect' (1 Cor. 2:6ff), does not refer to an abstract speculative gnosis, which is revealed to the initiated by the pneuma as a secret doctrine. The expression refers to the

knowledge of that which occurred in and with the 'historical'
Christ. This not only appears clearly from 1 Corinthians
2:7-8, but also in other places where Paul speaks of the
revelation of that which up until now had remained a hidden
mystery (Rom. 16:25-26; Eph. 3:5; Col. 1:25-27; Titus
1:2-3; 2 Tim. 1:10). 'To be hidden' is for Paul not an intel-
lectual or mystical category, but an historical category: That
which was hidden, *was not yet there;*[53] it was not yet realized
as the council and the promise of God. And the wisdom
which the Spirit reveals concerning the hiddenness of God
is, therefore, not a certain spiritual secret doctrine, but it is
the insight into that which occurred and was seen and heard
in and with Christ's coming (Cf. Matt. 13:11). Likewise,
the expression 'depths of God' which the Spirit examines,
does not refer to *das Innere und Innerste,*[54] but as Deiszner
has shown it has the same significance as in Romans 11:33,
and refers to the historical redemptive plans of God with
respect to the salvation realized in Christ.[55] The 'wisdom
of God' revealed by the Spirit therefore refers to a correct
appreciation of the cross of Christ. 1 Corinthians 2:6; 3:1-3
has been interpreted to mean that Paul makes a profound
distinction between the simple preaching of the cross, compared with milk to be served to children, and the doctrine
of wisdom, revealed by the pneuma to the 'perfected' adults.
However, it is to be remembered that already in 1 Corinthians 1:24 Paul contrasted the wisdom of the world with
the wisdom of God which consists of the *preaching of the
crucified Christ.* That which the Spirit reveals is, therefore, not some special source of knowledge and wisdom
to be distinguished from the historical *kerygma,* but it consists precisely in a correct distinction and understanding of
that which occurred in Christ's coming and work.[56] When
Paul appeals to the spirit of God for his own preaching, and
when he elsewhere attaches value to the particular working
of the Spirit and speaks of ecstasies and visions there is, in

this, not an independent principle of knowledge of the person and work of Christ, but it is rather the renewing and constructive work of the Holy Spirit, by which the preaching of the historical Christ receives its religious and moral application and effect.[57] Only in this sense is the Spirit to be understood as a principle providing knowledge of Christ and of the redemption sent in him (Cf. the close of the pneuma passage in 1 Cor. 2:16). "But we have the mind of Christ," i.e., the Spirit which comes from Christ and through which we can understand that which has been sent and revealed by God in Christ (vs. 16).

13. The Old Testament

One point to be noticed is Paul's repeated *appeal to the Old Testament,* when in the above mentioned sense he speaks of the mystery of God revealed in Christ (Cf. 1 Cor. 1:19; 2:16). This raises the question as to how far the Old Testament was a source of Paul's preaching of Christ.[58]

In general the essential character of Paul preaching of Christ can be seen clearly from the manner in which he brings the revelation of God in Christ and the Old Testament constantly in relation to each other. Nowhere is it more evident for Paul that Christ was not the proclaimer of a new idea, a new *ethos,* or a cultus-hero, in the sense of the then contemporary mystery religions. Paul's entire preaching is characterized by the conviction that Jesus is the Christ of Israel, and that, therefore, the coming and work of Christ can be understood only against the background of the history of the revelation which the Old Testament describes. Paul read the Scriptures and was convinced that the coming of Christ forms the provisional conclusion of the entire past divine redemptive work and that it must be understood as constituting an unbreakable coherence with the past. And on the basis of the unbreakable unity of the divine work,

Paul related Christ's coming and work to the great moments
in the Old Testament redemptive history (Adam, Abraham,
Moses, the Prophets) and sought its meaning against this
background.

Of special importance here is the well-known passage
of 2 Corinthians 3:12ff, where Paul speaks of a veil
(κάλυμμα)[59] which, in the reading of the Old Testament, is
laid over the hearts of the unbelieving Jews, and which can
only be removed by Christ. "But their minds were blinded
for until this day remaineth the same veil untaken away
in the reading of the Old Testament; which veil is done
away in Christ." "Nevertheless, when it shall turn to the
Lord the veil shall be taken away," vs. 16. Paul speaks here
of the glory of God's revelation, which the Jews incorrectly
still seek in the law, but which is now to be viewed in
Christ, and in the power of the Spirit, which in place of the
demand of the law, has been sent in Christ.[60] From this
it appears, however, that that which was revealed in the Old
Testament, of a provisional and passing glory, was already
the glory *of Christ*, and the Old Testament must now be
read from the present perspective of its fulfillment in Christ.
Therefore, Paul can write that the Old Testament Word of
God is written for us (δἰ ἡμᾶς) (Rom. 4:24; 1 Cor. 10:11),
and that "the Scripture, foreseeing that God would justify the
Gentiles through faith, preached before the gospel unto
Abraham" (Gal. 3:8). Moreover, the Scriptures therefore
contain the actual Word of God in that "they are written for
our admonition, upon whom the ends of the world are come"
(1 Cor. 10:11).

In this light Paul's Christological explanation of the Old
Testament is clear. It does not rest in Paul upon the subtlety
of the allegorical method, but upon the unity of the divine
redemptive work,[61] and therefore it finds its limits and norms
in the revelation of Jesus Christ. The pre-history of the
redemption in Israel is determined by the future. There-

fore, Christ is also present in the old covenant, and Paul can say of the rock in the wilderness, out of which Israel received water, that this is Christ (1 Cor. 10:4). And likewise he can say that Christ died for our sins, according to the Scriptures, that he was buried and on the third day arose again (1 Cor. 15:3-4). Thus, there is a connection between the curse by which God threatened his people in the days of old, and the curse which Christ has borne (Gal. 3:13) and the promise to Abraham is spoken to Christ (Gal. 3:16). The deeds and mercy of God's grace in the Old Testament are for Paul not thinkable apart from Christ (Rom. 4:6). In fact the entire revelation of God has a relationship to Christ (Rom. 10:15-18). Masson correctly applies the frequently used formula of Paul in Christ, ἐν χριστῷ, to his reading of the Old Testament.[62] The entire history of salvation of the old covenant receives its meaning for Paul only in the coming of Christ and was only written according to its broad historical redemptive vision with an eye on those who in the future would believe in Christ (Rom. 15:4).

Paul's preaching of Christ is not thinkable without taking the Old Testament into account. However, this must not be conceived of in such a way that the Old Testament becomes for Paul a means of arriving at all sorts of speculative views concerning the person and work of Christ. The only thing that Paul does in his Christological exegesis of the Old Testament is to point to the sources and to delineate the course which finds its fulfillment in the New Testament revelation.

The swelling stream of the unity of God's redemptive action is the starting point of Paul's view of history and the principle of his scriptural exegesis. It forms a complete antithesis to any immanent causal conception of the people of Israel, and of the so-called Israelite literature, and it is also opposed to idealistic speculative Christology. Paul's Christology also in its sources is of a redemptive historical character. We shall seek to demonstrate this in the following.

In summary, with respect to the sources of Paul's preaching of Christ, the direct data of the New Testament points before everything else to the revelation which Paul received from the risen, exalted Christ, and to the tradition received from the early Christian church. This does not deny but rather presupposes that his preaching bears the stamp of his own personality, spiritual gifts, and theological powers. Nevertheless, in spite of all these personal, penetrating, and unique characteristics, and even a one-sided emphasis, Paul is, in the most absolute sense of the word, aware that he is a legitimate proclaimer of the historical Jesus Christ, and that he is in full harmony with his fellow apostles, and is also in a direct continuous relationship with the Old Testament revelation. Moreover, Paul passionately opposes any falsification of the gospel, and appeals to the leading of the Spirit of Christ in support of his conception of the wisdom of God.

CHAPTER IV

THE GENERAL CHARACTER
OF PAUL'S PREACHING OF CHRIST

14. *The Perspective of the History of Redemption (Heils-geschichte)*

To deal with the actual content of the Pauline *kerygma,* and to give a general characterization of it, the eschatological or rather the *heilsgeschichtliche* interpretation has in many ways made a more correct view possible. The improvement is not only to be noted in comparison with modern views of Paul but also with respect to views held during the Reformation period. Under the influence of the basic theme of the Reformation, justification by faith was for a long time viewed as the actual content of Paul's gospel, around which all the other elements of his epistles were grouped.[1] Our objection is not that such a notion attaches too great an importance to justification by faith, as has repeatedly been affirmed by the liberal and the *religionsgeschichtliche school.* Justification by faith unmistakably belongs to the very heart of Paul's preaching, and is not a secondary 'polemic' directed against the Jews (Wrede[2]), or a 'side issue' within the main stream of the mystical doctrine of redemption of 'being in Christ' (Schweitzer[3]). But by approaching Paul's doctrine exclusively from the standpoint of justification by faith there is a danger of depriving Paul's preaching of its redemptive historical dynamic and of making it into a timeless treatment of the vital question: how is one justified before God? Justification by faith as proclaimed by Paul is rather one *aspect,* although a very central aspect, of the great redemptive event of which Paul knew himself to be the herald, and which he described as the fulness of time in which God has sent the Son (Gal. 4:4), as the revelation of the mystery that has been hid for ages and from generations (Rom. 11:25-26; Col. 1:26), as the grace, which is given to us in Jesus Christ before the world began, but is now made manifest by the appearing of our Saviour Jesus Christ (2 Tim. 1:9-10), so that it can now be said, old things are passed away; behold all things are become new (2 Cor. 5:17); behold, now is the accepted time, behold now is the day of salvation (2 Cor. 6:2).

The importance of this viewpoint for a correct understanding of the general character of Paul's preaching appears, when we realize all the conceptions of criticism concerning the real core of Paul's preaching. First, the contrast between the flesh and spirit, then the mystical communion with Christ was conceived of as the dominating motif of his preaching. Paul has been viewed as a Hegelian idealist (Tübingen school), as a preacher of the superiority of the human spirit (the liberals); as a mystic of the Hellenistic mystery-religions (Bousset); as a gnostic, par excellence (Reitzenstein). And as a result the 'religion' of Paul was placed at such a great distance from that of Jesus that the cleft was apparently unbridgeable. What was forgotten, however, in all these changing conceptions and interpretations of Paul, was the awareness that Paul's preaching was not formed by a new idea, or by a new ethos, or a new religious vital feeling or a *Seinsverständnis,* but before everything else, he was the *proclaimer of a new time,* the great turning point in the history of redemption, the intrusion of a new world aeon. Such was the dominating perspective and foundation of Paul's entire preaching. It alone can illuminate the many facets and interrelations of his preaching, e.g., justification, being-in-Christ, suffering, dying, and rising again with Christ, the conflict between the spirit and the flesh, the cosmic drama, etc.

The person of Jesus Christ forms the mystery and the middle point of this great historical redemptive revelation. Because Christ is revealed a new aeon has been ushered in, the old world has ended, and the new world has begun. Paul's entire doctrine of redemption is, therefore, in all its aspects, a proclamation and explication of the redemption which has come in Christ as the fulfillment of salvation. Paul's eschatology is messianology, Christology. But on the other hand, Paul's preaching of Christ is only understood correctly when viewed in all its dramatic force as the disclosure of the hiddenness of the redemptive history, as the actual preaching of the long expected day of salvation.[4] The merit of the eschatological interpretation of the New Testament is that in opposition to the liberal and *religionsgeschichtliche* school it again brought to the fore this dominating motif.

This perspective is not only of great importance for a correct view of Paul's preaching, but also for the question which concerns us primarily: the relationship between Jesus and Paul. When compared with that of Jesus, Paul's preaching has been recognized by many, in spite of its entirely different form, to be in essence simply the expression of what Jesus referred to when he spoke of the kingdom of heaven being at hand. Paul, in his own way, is the preacher, to the Jews and the Greeks, of the entrance of the eschatological redemptive period, promised by God and proclaimed by Jesus. And, as in the *kerygma* of the gospels, and the witness of the early church, the person and the work of Jesus forms the proper content of the coming of this kingdom, so also Paul is the preacher and the herald of Jesus as the Christ, in whom the salvation promised by God is disclosed.

From this perspective can be understood what for many is often a stumbling block; that Paul's preaching reflects so little of Jesus' commands and parables and concentrates instead upon the cross and resurrection of Christ. This has given rise to all sorts of alleged conflicts between Jesus and Paul. Jesus is thought to be the preacher of God's universal fatherly love of all mankind; and Paul, in contrast, is thought to have mixed this simple doctrine of love with various Jewish juridical elements and to have made it into a propitiatory theology of blood. The *heilsgeschichtliche* approach has cleared up a great many misunderstandings with respect to the preaching of Jesus and Paul. When it is understood that the preaching of Jesus and of Paul is primarily concerned with the entrance of the redemptive period promised by God, of which the person of Jesus forms the explanation and the central point, it is then clear that the entire soteriology of the original gospel of Jesus, as well as that of Paul, is based upon what occurred in and to the person of Jesus as the Christ. The new redemptive proclamation rests from the very beginning—and that is what distinguishes it, for example, from the Old Testament proclamation of redemption—*upon the new redemptive facts*. When therefore Paul's preaching finds its central point in the death and resurrection of Christ, this is not because Paul did not have any knowledge of Jesus' commandments or attach significance to them, but because in Christ's death and resurrection, the *heilsgeschichtliche* drama of Christ's coming and work reached its highest point. God's promise of redemption reached its completion in the most profound and wonderful fact that prior to the resurrection his redeemer must suffer death, and be subject to the powers of men and demons. Paul's conceptions are focused upon this mystery and its disclosure. Not because Paul was influenced by the myths of the mystery cults, or by any other mythological drama, as the *religionsgeschichtliche* school would have us believe, but because within the cadre of the Christian era, which had just begun, nothing else was of such decisive significance as the death and resurrection of Christ. One does not need to seek the influences of alien motives. Given the fact that Jesus was the Christ, and that with his coming the kingdom had arrived; given the historical redemptive significance of Jesus' person and work, then the decisive moment could only have been the moment when Jesus was first delivered unto death, and was later resurrected by the omnipotence of God.

This fundamental agreement between Paul's preaching of Christ and Jesus' self-revelation permits the question as to how far Jesus' and Paul's preaching represent and bear the mark of different stages in the progress of this great redemptive event. In the preceding we have been opposed to the deeply penetrating reconstruction of the gospel of the radical eschatological interpretation, according to which Jesus based his point of view upon the pre-messianic standpoint of proclamation and expectation, and Paul in contrast stood upon that of messianic fulfillment. We do not wish at this point to abandon any part of our former position. *The basic motif of the entire New Testament kerygma is that of the fulfillment of the historical redemption which began with Christ's coming.* And Jesus himself is the ground and origin of this view of history, because of his preaching of the kingdom of God, and also because of his messianic self-revelation.[5] In this respect Paul does not originate anything which is new in principle. And this is not only true of the entrance of the fulfillment, but also of its provisional character as is so clearly indicated by Jesus.[6] In spite of the great degree of emphasis Paul placed upon the *revelation* of the mystery, of the fulness of time, which he places in the foreground, and considers to have its inception and fulfillment with the coming of Christ in the flesh (Gal. 4:4), undoubtedly this revelation also bore a provisional character for Paul. It is just the peculiar tension between the certainty of that which occurred and the expectation of that which must still occur which forms the focal point of the *kerygma,* retained within his apostolic writings (Rom. 8; 1 Cor. 15).

The fact still remains, however, that Jesus' preaching represents the stage in the history of the gospel before the resurrection, and Paul—even as the early Christian church—looks back to the resurrection as the highest point of the revelation of the divine mystery. It is in such terms that the peculiar differences of Jesus' and Paul's preaching can be explained. What we have said is especially true with respect to the significance of Jesus' own person and work. Jesus' self-revelation, especially in the synoptic gospels, is still in many respects characterized by a certain amount of reserve and hiddenness, and even the meaning of his suffering and death is kept in the background. But, in Paul's preaching there is a great eulogy to the salvation accomplished in Christ's death and resurrection, and Paul wrestles with language to find words lofty enough to glorify the risen Christ. Because of the latter aspect it is frequently held that Paul's Christology is scarcely related to the historical Jesus, that he showed little or no interest in Jesus 'according to the flesh' and he assimilated, moreover, the death and resurrection of Christ entirely in a pneumatic Christology (Cf. Rom. 6:1-14). We shall subsequently examine this conception in more detail. Here it ought to be noticed in general that such a view misunderstands the redemptive historical starting point of Paul's preaching. The basic attitude of Paul's gospel—if such can be spoken of—is dominated by the redemptive facts, by that which occurred in Christ. Therefore, any attempt to detach the connection between Paul's Christology and history is an attack upon the very heart of Paul's preaching. Nevertheless, for Paul this history is not simply a holy past which is at an end and to which one simply looks back. The One who once came to earth, suffered and died is risen again and exalted to the right hand of God, he is the living Lord, who now works through the Spirit, within the church and in the apostles. In this sense, Paul can say: "Wherefore henceforth know we no man after the flesh: yea, though we have known Christ after the flesh, yet now henceforth know we know him no more" (2 Cor. 5:16). This is not a devaluation of the historical in order to substitute in its place a timeless pneumatic element. It is simply the recognition that everything that Jesus did and spoke on earth is now determined for the church by and through his resurrection; it indicates that the *perfectum* is a *perfectum praesens*. What Paul proclaims concerning Jesus are not *memorabilia* out of a dead past, but it is the way along which Jesus Christ became what he now is; it is the stroke of victory, which is now celebrated. In the redemptive facts of the past lie the explanation of the redemptive situation of the present. Therefore, they form the foundation of Paul's entire proclamation. But it is not the figure of Jesus who once wandered through the fields of Galilee, nor is it the historical picture of the Nazarene, which forms the content of Paul's preaching; but it is the living Lord, who has been exalted out of his humiliation, and who as such is now the Lord of the church. Herein lies a difference from what comes to the fore in Jesus' own preaching and self-revelation before his resurrection. For now is revealed what then was still hidden; now that is preached from the housetops, what then was whispered in the ear (Mark 4:22; Matt. 10:27). Yet this does not say that Paul preached a different Jesus than the Jesus according to the flesh. Paul preached the same Christ, but Paul now proclaims a Jesus who died, and rose again, and who now sits at the right hand of God, the Father. The difference does not lie in the fact that the one picture is historical and human, whereas the other is super-historical and divine; but it lies in the fact that the history of redemption had progressed, that the Christ according to the flesh is now the Lord of the heavens. It is in principle the fact of the resurrection that determines, in its continuing redemptive historical significance, Paul's preaching of Jesus, and distinguishes it from Jesus' original messianic self-revelation.[7]

Our subject has not yet been dealt with exhaustively. The principle and material agreement between Jesus' self-revelation and Paul's preaching comes to light when one views both from the standpoint of the fulfillment of redemptive history. Nevertheless, the question remains, whether that which Paul teaches within this framework concerning the person and work of Christ was already present in Jesus' self-revelation and can therefore be deduced with justification.

Even though it is impossible in this short discussion to give an exhaustive examination of the revelant passages of Paul, we must in this context deal with those passages concerned with the divine glorification of Christ's person and the all-inclusive significance of his work. It is especially with respect to these main points of Paul's Christology that the old question 'Jesus and Paul' continues to be of actual significance in modern literature. To see this question in its proper perspective it is necessary that we briefly examine the content of Paul's epistles which is here relevant.

15. The Person and Work of Christ

In the first place the glorification which Paul ascribes to Jesus as the Christ does not have a bearing only on Christ's resurrection and exaltation. Therefore, Paul speaks of the latter as the acceptance of Christ's unlimited domination. The *locus classicus* is here Philippians 2:9-11, in which in particular the name *Kyrios* (Lord) forms the basis of Christ's power over the entire cosmos. This divine resurrection glory, which as we have seen characterizes the preaching of Paul in distinction from Jesus' earthly self-revelation is, however, not the sole factor which must here be discussed. Paul also con-

Pree
Chst

PAUL'S PREACHING OF CHRIST 71

tinually speaks of Christ's pre-existent glory as that of the Son of God, and without any reservation considers it one of the most fundamental and indisputable parts of the faith of the church. Thus, for example, in Galatians 4:4, "But when the fulness of time was come, God sent forth his Son," it is implied that Christ in his pre-existent life already was the Son of God (Cf. also Rom. 1:3; 8:3).[8] Elsewhere he speaks in greater detail both of this pre-existence and of the significance of this sonship. See especially Philippians 2:6ff and Colossians 1:15ff, which are here of importance. In Philippians 2, it is said of Christ that he was in the form of God and thought it not robbery to be equal with God. Now even if one believes that these expressions in Paul require a poetic interpretation,[9] and not a strictly termino-logical explanation, it is nevertheless not to be denied that the expression 'in the form of God' discloses Christ's divine glory and points to his equality with God. The expression 'being equal with God' gives another description of this same state of affairs without speaking of it as a higher condition,[10] which Christ would have been able to acquire if he had wished. Both expressions refer to Christ's divine majesty,[11] as the pre-existent Son of God. In 2 Corinthians 8:9, this is expressed with the simple words that Christ 'though he was rich' became poor for our sakes. Elsewhere, in 2 Corinthians 4:4, and especially in Colossians 1:15ff, we find similar references to Christ's glorification. He is the 'image of God,' 'the image of the invisible God.'[12] These expressions also signify that Christ, as the Son of God, is the disclosure, the expression of God himself. It is not here a question of a weakening or an imitation of the divine glory but the refer-ence is rather to the revelation of the divine glory.

All this is said of Christ, as the pre-existent Son of God, as is especially evident from the sequence of Colos-sians 1:15.[13] In these passages, as in 1 Corinthians 8:6, participation in a divine creative work is ascribed to Christ,

and he is spoken of as the one who is the first born of all
creatures, that is to say the first in relationship to all that has
been created.[14] Christ is not a creature relegated to the side
of creation. But he is on the side of God, the first born,
as also "for by Him are all things created. . . . " And he is
before all things, and by him all things consist, vss. 16-17.
This cosmic significance of Christ in his pre-existence now
finds its counterpart in his redemptive work. As he is the
first born with respect to all creatures, so he is also the first
born of the dead, and as everything has existence in him,
so also is he the one by whom the entire cosmos, everything upon the earth as well as everything in heaven, is
again reconciled to God. Especially in the 'cosmic pronouncements' about Christ, is Paul's preaching of an unspeakable
scope. Christ's work includes not only the heavens and the
earth but it embraces also the creation and its complete
consummation. In him dwells the fulness of God (Cf. vs.
19; 2:9).

In the light of these passages it is not surprising that
Paul's entire preaching, also for the present, is characterized
by the recognition of the absolute equality and unity between
Christ and the Father. Everything which is ascribed to God
is ascribed also to Christ. Paul prays to him (2 Cor. 12:8-9);
his name is 'called upon' in the church (1 Cor. 1:2; Rom.
10:13), an expression, which in the Old Testament is repeatedly employed for God; one expects of him that which
only God has the power to send (Rom. 1:7; 1 Cor. 1:3;
2 Cor. 1:2; Eph. 1:2; Rom. 16:10; 2 Cor. 13:13); to him
is the same honor ascribed as to God (Cf. Phil. 2:10 with
Rom. 14:11); the footstool of Christ is spoken of as the judgment seat of God, (Cf. Rom. 14:10 with 2 Cor. 5:10); Christ's
gospel, his kingdom, his spirit, are spoken of as that of God
(Cf. Rom. 1:1 with Rom. 15:16; Eph. 5:5; Rom. 8:9).[15]

Paul says also of him in the explicit sense that he is God
(2 Thess. 1:12, "The grace of our God and Lord Jesus

Christ"[16] and Tit. 2:13, "The glorious appearing of the great
God and our saviour Jesus Christ").[17]   Also Romans 9:5,
"Christ, who is above all, God bless him forever," from a
linguistic point of view, ought to be exegeted to mean that
Christ *expressis verbis* is here called God.[18]   In view of statements of glorification which Paul elsewhere ascribes to
Christ, there is nothing strange or impossible in this interpretation, even though it is understandable that the apostle
seldom makes use of this predicate, when applying it to
Christ, because, in general, when unqualified the expression
refers to God the Father, and there is naturally no question
of an identity of the person of the Father and that of Christ.
The pronouncements in Paul's epistles concerning Christ's
human nature ought also to be understood in the light of
this glorification-Christology.   When Paul speaks of Jesus'
earthly life this always occurs against the background of
the pre-existent glorification of the Son of God, and never
solely against the background of Jesus' human, earthly birth.
From this the conclusion is incorrectly drawn that in Paul
the earthly, historical Jesus is entirely transformed into a
supernatural heavenly being, whose temporal earthly life,
if not understood in a docetical sense, is still of little significance for Paul's own (pneumatic) Christology.   There cannot be an uncertainty that the content of Paul's gospel
consists in the historical revelation of the Son of God,
in his coming in the fulness of time, in his death, resurrection, and exaltation.   It is also true that the aim of
Paul's preaching does not consist in a profound description
of Christ's divine being or essence but only in the redemptive
proclamation of his work.   All this does not remove the
fact, however, that the significance of that *which Christ did*
has its basis in that which he *was* and *is* and that one may
therefore not detach the Christological *ereignis* categories
from the ontological categories.   This is, therefore, also the
reason that the incarnation and the human nature of Christ

in Paul's epistles, are always viewed as a wonder of divine
grace and not as a natural event.

That Christ in the full sense of the word was born as
a man among man, that he lived, suffered, and died is
in Paul's proclamation of the gospel just as indisputable
as his pre-existent glory. Also this can be pointed out
from Galatians 4:4, where of the Son of God it is said:
"When the fulness of time was come, God sent forth his
Son, born out of a woman, made under the law." Both the
preposition, out (ἐκ not διά) and the undetermined expression, 'a woman' indicate the absolute connection and
unity of Christ with mankind (Cf. Job 14:1; Matt. 11:11).
The woman was not only the means or organ of his coming
into the flesh but from her he took everything which is
proper to mankind. Therefore, he was also 'under the law'
as a man among man. Even so in Romans 1:3 (Cf. 2 Tim.
2:8), it is said of the Son of God that he was "born out of
the seed of David, according to the flesh." Also here it
appears that the expression: 'born out of' does not only
indicate a temporal belonging to or solidarity with David's
issue, but also indicates his origin in this family. The words
'according to the flesh' can be conceived of as a limiting
circumscription in order to indicate that Christ was also a
participant in another mode of existence (Cf. vs. 4).[19] That
Christ was thus spoken of 'according to the flesh' includes
the fact, however, that he entered into human existence and
that his existence is also thereby determined.[20] The term
'flesh' does not only refer to the physical but also to his entire
human existence. On the basis of these passages there
cannot be any doubt even for a moment that Christ was
born, lived, and died as a man in the full sense of the word.
A close examination reveals again and again how much the
apostle had wrestled with the language to bring to expression
the divine mystery of the incarnation of the Son of God.
Thus, for example, in Romans 8:3, where he says that God

sent his Son in the likeness[21] of sinful flesh, the expression
'in the likeness' does not point in a docetical direction,[22] but
simply indicates that it cannot be said without qualification
that Christ had taken on a human existence qualified by sin.
One can then also not understand these words in the sense
that Christ actually bore the sinful flesh and that Christ's
flesh, even as our own was condemned for sin.[23] We must
rather understand this expression in terms of Paul's conviction of Christ's absolute sinlessness (2 Cor. 5:21). Whereas
the empirical human existence must be characterized as
'sinful flesh,' as an existence that is entirely controlled by sin,
Christ had no part in this sin, even though, at the same time,
in every other respect he is, nevertheless, not to be distinguished from other men, and therefore was in his flesh
uniquely able to bear the punishment of sin.[24]

Also in this connection the well-known passage in Philippians 2, verses 6-11 must be understood. After that which is
said of Christ's pre-existent, divine glory,[25] there follows
that Christ "made himself of no reputation, and took upon
himself the form of a servant, and was made in the likeness of man; and being found and fashioned as a man,
he humbled himself and became obedient unto death, even
the death of the cross." Insofar as these words have any
relationship to Christ's incarnation and human nature they
state in the first place that Christ has humbled himself. The
expression ἐκένωσεν, which has been the cause of many
a dogmatic conflict,[26] does not say anything more in itself
than that the Christ, who is described in the preceding, laid
aside his divine glory (Cf. 2 Cor. 8:9). That he thereby did
not cease to be who he was, the pre-existent eternal Son of
God, is in this context as self evident[27] as the fact that he did
not only hide this divine glory.[28] The latter is also the import
of the threefold way in which his human nature is described:
as 'assuming the form of a slave'—in contrast with being in
the form of God—which here also is not a pronouncement

concerning Christ's being or nature, but a statement of the manner of his revelation, of the modality of his entrance into the world. In our opinion the two following circumscriptions speak more directly of the incarnation. The expression which we have translated by the word 'was made in the likeness of man' contains the same word as Romans 8:3.[29] That here is spoken of 'the likeness of men' and not simply of 'a man' finds its reason not in the fact that the reference is only to a *similarity* (Rom. 8:3, see above), but might be explained as in opposition to 'being in the form of God.'[30] What is spoken of here is not simply the fact that he was a man (even though this is also presupposed), but it is concerned with the manner of his being *a man* in contrast to his divine glory.[31]

The last expression "being found and fashioned as a man" speaks of Christ's taking action[32] as a man. The expression 'as' not only expresses a relationship of similarity but also of identity. In his entire manner of acting he shows himself to be what he also was, a man. The word 'as' simply lays emphasis upon the modality of Christ's entry. It is of course certain that all these difficult expressions are based upon Christ's human nature.[33] However, it is not human nature itself that here receives the emphasis, but the humiliation of Christ implied in the fact that the Son of God became a man.

Paul's preaching of Christ's redemptive work must be seen in connection with the thus conceived divine glorification and humiliation of Christ, as the Son of God. One can say that everything centers around the significance of Christ's crucifixion and resurrection (1 Cor. 1:18ff; 2:2; 15:3;[34] Gal. 6:14; Rom. 4:25ff), and the redemptive significance of this is explicitly described by Paul in such general and particular terms as 'ransoming' (1 Cor. 6:20; 7:23; Gal. 3:13; 4:5), 'reconciliation' (2 Cor. 5:18ff; Rom. 5:10ff; Eph. 2:16; Col. 1:20ff); 'justification' (Rom. 4:25; 5:19, etc.).

Even though it is not possible to direct our attention in this context to the richness, diversity, and the many sidedness of the ideas contained here,[35] we ought to emphasize one point: that the entire redemptive work must be viewed against the background of Christ's pre-existent glory, as the Son of God who descended from heaven and ascended again into heaven. This redemption thereby acquires the significance of an all-inclusive divine drama, of a cosmic struggle, in which is involved not only man in his sin and lost condition, but in which are also related the heavens and the earth, angels and demons, and the goal of which is to bring back the entire created cosmos under God's dominion and rule. All this appears very clearly from the passages cited from Colossians 1. From the fact that Christ is both the author of creation, and the re-creation, the conclusion is drawn that by his crucifixion he has reconciled everything upon the earth and all that which is in the heavens (1:20), whereby in this context the term 'reconciliation' acquires the significance of: being brought into a right relationship with God.[36] Likewise, in Colossians 2:13, it is said that Christ "having spoiled principalities and powers he made a show of them openly, triumphing over them in it." And even though it is not easy in this respect to form an exact conception of what the apostle meant by the terms 'principalities and powers,'[37] it is clear that the redemptive work of Christ is not only human and earthly but that it has much broader dimensions, in that the entire invisible world of spirits is related to it. In short, the commission which Christ had to execute can be understood in its full significance only against the background of the conflict between God and Satan. Even though 'the principles of the world'[38] of which Paul writes in Galatians 4:3 and Colossians 2:20 may not be understood in this sense,[39] there is in Paul's epistles corresponding to the ontical and cosmic statements about Christ's person, a great conception of Christ's redemptive work. The glorification,

78 PAUL AND JESUS

which Christ according to Paul's preaching received after his
exaltation thereby acquires a pregnant sense, for example
in Ephesians 1:20-21, when it is said that God set him
at his own right hand in the heavenly places, far above
all principalities, and power, and might, and dominion,
and every name that is named, not only in this world, but
also in that which is to come," and when it is said in Philippians 2:10ff that at the name of Jesus every knee should bow,
of things in heaven, and things on earth, and things under
the earth, and that every tongue should confess that Jesus
Christ is Lord! All this reflects the all-inclusive character
of Christ's coming to earth, of his death and resurrection,
and brings to light that, as the Son of God not only in creation, but also in the redemption, and the completion of the
world, all things are given in his hands. And, therefore,
only against this background can a correct insight be
acquired into Christ's existence and work as a man upon
the earth.

It has been observed that it is especially on the basis
of this more exact characterization of Paul's preaching of
Christ that the problem 'Jesus and Paul' has remained a
problem, even for those who in opposition to the liberal and
religionsgeschichtliche school maintain the basic eschatological motive of Jesus' and of Paul's preaching. It is true that
Albert Schweitzer believes that this Pauline Christology—
insofar as he accepts its genuineness[40]—can entirely or nearly
be reduced to the late Jewish apocalyptic messianology,[41] so
that Paul also in this respect did nothing but bring the
'eschatological dogma' which also controlled Jesus' preaching, to its logical conclusion. Usually, however, it is held
that what Paul predicated in the aforementioned sense of
the person and the work of Christ, far exceeded the traditional Jewish messianology in many respects, even in its
transcendent apocalyptic form. The latter point of view is
in our opinion irrefutable. For even if the idea of the

pre-existent Son of Man could be derived from the Jewish apocalypse,[42] the idea of the deity and of the incarnation of the Son of Man, in the sense in which Paul speaks of it, is a conception entirely foreign to Jewish writings. Likewise, there is in the latter nothing to be found of the notion of the participation of the Messiah in the creation of the world.[43] The attempt to explain Paul's Christology as a modification of the late Jewish messianology must be viewed then as a complete failure.

Many still will not recognize Paul's preaching of Christ as a purely Christian phenomenon, which is solely dependent upon Jesus' self-revelation, and the faith of the early church. Especially with respect to Paul's Christological views, his preaching is thought to be a syncretistic conglomeration of Jewish-eschatological, and Hellenistic gnostic motives. This synthesis of the eschatological and *religionsgeschichtliche* interpretation of Paul's Christology today finds its most prominent and most radical expression in Bultmann's *Theology of the New Testament*. Bultmann believes that the Hellenistic influences upon the eschatological foundations of Paul's preaching of Christ can be established on four points:

1. In his preaching of Christ as *the pneumatic Kyrios;*
2. In his preaching of Christ as *ontical Son of God;*
3. In his preaching of Christ's *descent from the heavens;*
4. In his preaching of Christ's *cosmic significance* both in the work of creation and in that of redemption.

In our discussion of these four basic motifs in Paul's preaching of Christ we shall not simply be negative but we shall try to reach a positive conclusion with respect to the relationship between Paul's proclamation, Jesus' self-revelation and the faith of the early church based upon the latter.

CHAPTER V

PAUL, THE EARLY CHRISTIAN CHURCH, AND JESUS

16. Kyrios Christus

The first important difference which criticism would point out between Paul's Christology and that of the early Christian church and, in a still stronger degree between Paul and Jesus, is related to the character of Christ's exaltation. The early church supposedly still thought in Jewish-eschatological categories and conceived of Jesus as the Son of Man, who in keeping with Daniel 7 is clothed with all power in heaven, and whose *parousia* as world-judge would soon come about. In the case of Paul, however, the Hellenistic Christianity supposedly came to its full expression, accompanied by the pneumatic conception of Christ's being in the heavens. The title 'Christ' no longer refers to the messianic-eschatological office but has entirely become a proper name. In contrast the characteristic element of Paul's faith in Christ finds its expression in the title *Kyrios*. As in the Hellenistic mystery cults, the deity is evoked with the title 'Lord,' thus also the name *Kyrios* in Paul's preaching became the indication of the pneumatic character that his Christology bore in imitation of that of the Hellenistic cultus-gathering (especially at Antioch). Jesus Christ is no longer expected in the future as the world judge, but he is expected in the cult as the pneumatic *Kyrios,* into whose fellowship one rises through ecstasy, mysticism, and spiritual gifts, and who for Paul is also the origin of the

individual moral life of faith. This theory, which was defended by Bousset, is repeated by Bultmann, insofar as he
thinks that the Hellenistic Christianity of Paul represents
something new, in contrast to the Palestinian, and insofar
as Paul's Christianity belongs to the sphere of the mystery
religions and of the gnosis, and as such can be described
by the name *Kyrios*.[1]

Now this theory concerning the origin of the name
Kyrios, as constructed by Bousset, and advanced by many,
is for the most part no longer acceptable to most scholars,[2]
and the attempt of Bultmann to give new life to it can hardly
be viewed as successful. It has become clear that when Paul
calls Christ 'the Lord,' he does not think in terms of the
Hellenistic mystery cults, but this usage is firmly related
to the eschatological messianic faith of the early Palestinian
church, which was based upon Jesus' self-revelation.

However, before we proceed further, we must first
briefly deal with the terminological arguments which can be
advanced against this view.[3]

a. The name *Kyrios* is with respect to its origin not to
be understood as referring only to the Hellenistic cultus
heroes, but rather as the Greek term which refers to the
general semitic conception of the deity as king and ruler.[4]
In the LXX (Septuagint) *Kyrios* is the usual translation of
'Jahwe.' The use of this title for Jesus does not necessarily
have to be viewed as a conscious transfer of the Old Testament name of God, but it can thus be understood as a
reference to Jesus' messianic glory, which rests on a much
broader basis. The name *Kyrios* when used of Jesus certainly does not arise out of the cults, but out of the prophetic-
eschatological sphere. It refers to the divine character of
Christ's exalted, royal status. That Judaism had never described the Messiah as the 'Lord'[5] does not serve as a counter
argument. Jesus' messianic glorification, as this was confessed by the church, from the very beginning after his

resurrection, far exceeded the Jewish conceptions concerning the Messiah. Even in the gospels (by an appeal to Psalm 110), reference is made to the glory of the Messiah which far exceeds the Jewish conceptions (Cf. Mark 12:35ff). In this Psalm the name 'Lord' indicates the messianic king ordained by God (David's Son, and David's Lord). The fact that in Jewish linguistic usage the absolute, 'the Lord,' as it appears in Paul, is not thinkable, but must receive a narrower specification (e.g., 'Our Lord') does not prove that the title 'Lord,' as applied by Paul to Jesus, cannot be of semitic origin. From the frequent predicative usage, which also appears in Paul, an absolute usage can well arise. The Greek linguistic usage may have advanced this absolute usage.[6] In any case, the Hellenistic cultus origin of the *Kyrios* title, as applied to Jesus, cannot be proved in this manner.

b. From the sources themselves it is evident that the *Kyrios* title appeared in the earliest church. That it seldom appears in the synoptic gospels, and then frequently in the sense of 'master' or 'rabbi,' is not strange. However, if the *Kyrios* title is mainly a predicate applicable to the risen exalted Lord, it is obvious that in the oldest parts of the tradition, it would not be applied to Jesus in his earthly appearance[7] at all, or only very seldom. Yet within the synoptic gospels important points of contact are present for later usage, for example, when something is desired of Jesus that far exceeds his office as a teacher, he is addressed by the title 'Lord' (Cf. Matt. 8:25; Luke 5:8). Moreover Jesus also used the formula "the Lord hath need of it" (Matt. 21:3ff).[8] Further, one can point to such passages as Matthew 7:21, "Not everyone that sayeth unto me Lord! Lord! shall enter into the kingdom of heaven," and Mark 12:35-37 (David's Son and David's Lord). It is true that Bousset and others explain such a passage as Matthew 7:21 as secondary (i.e., a result of later Christological developments), even as the relevant passages in Acts (especially Acts 2:36)!

But it is difficult to deny that in proceeding in such a fashion one uses hypotheses rather than the sources themselves as the criteria of truth and genuineness, and in this fashion one postulates that which ought to be proven.[9]

c. One of the strongest counter arguments against Bousset's theory is that Paul himself employs the name 'Lord' in Aramaic (1 Cor. 16:22): 'Maranatha!' (Our Lord, come!), (Cf. also Did. 10:6). Bousset tried to deprive this argument of its force by pointing out that the area of the Hellenistic church at Damascus and Antioch was bilingual and that this Maranatha-formula could have originated very well in this Hellenistic group.[10] Bultmann gives another solution. In his opinion this eschatological supplication certainly originates in the early church, but this does not afford any proof that the early church appealed to Jesus as the Lord: "for it could have originally been applied to God, although it later was also used to refer to Jesus" (Cf. Rev. 22:20).[11] This argumentation is, however, very speculative and it cannot remove the force of the argument derived from 1 Corinthians 16:22. That Paul in a letter to the Greek church at Corinth made use of this formula can only be explained in terms of its original usage in the predominately early Jewish church.[12] To affirm that this original form did not have any reference to Jesus but only to God is not only undemonstrable but it can serve only with difficulty as a counter argument. Paul employs this word in any case as a Christological formula employed by the Aramaic speaking church, as a word of the church used in the period before the Greek language was the language used to spread the gospel. Therefore, on the basis of this prayer formula it can be said correctly: "In the early Palestinian church lies the origin of the application of the title of Lord, the κύριος title, to Jesus, which title subsequently received its deepest and most comprehensive meaning in Paul, especially in the antithesis to the κύριοι of the Hellenistic world."[13]

d. In opposition to the position we have stated, the argument has little force that the term *Kyrios* came about after the messianic title 'Son of Man' and 'Christ' (the term Christ then would only have the value of a proper name), were no longer in usage. Concerning the name 'Christ' it can be stated that it retained its full messianic significance for Paul and this can be deduced from the fact that Paul frequently, in reverse order, speaks of Christ Jesus,[14] and also from the connection which Paul repeatedly lays between his preaching of Christ and the Old Testament. Jesus remains for him in the first place, the Christ of Israel.[15] And, moreover, concerning the name 'the Son of Man,' it may be true that this name was difficult to understand in the Hellenistic churches and therefore, was not used or was used seldom, but this is also true of the early church at Jerusalem as far as we can judge from the sources. It can hardly be accidental that this name, with one exception (Acts 7:56), is used exclusively in the New Testament as a self description of Jesus, and then not only in the gospels directed to the Jews, but also in the gospels directed to the pagans. All this points to the historical determination of the use of the term, employed by Jesus to designate himself. It may be difficult to explain with complete certainty the fact that it practically comes to the fore only in Jesus' own mouth.[16] But in any case its less frequent usage or even the complete lack of usage cannot be used to prove an eradication of eschatological consciousness. That the latter remained appears clearly from the first chapters of Acts, where the life of the church is completely dominated by the dramatic tension of the redemptive historical events, which took place in Christ's death and resurrection, without the name 'the Son of Man' being employed by the church as a title of the resurrected Lord.

Now even if one disregards the terminological aspect and looks at the matter itself the opinion appears untenable that the name *Kyrios* indicates a transition from the Palestinian (which is based upon Jesus' self-revelation) to Hellenistic Christianity. When Paul uses the term *Kyrios* to refer to Christ's heavenly glory, this does not mean that his dynamic, historical expectation of Christ has been replaced by a mystical worship of Christ. To refute this notion no other appeal is necessary than to the *locus classicus* of the Pauline usage of the name *Kyrios* (Phil. 2:11). In this passage the name of honor *Kyrios* is used to describe the reward of the humiliation which Christ took upon himself, and as an indication of the exaltation which had already begun, but which was also still to be further manifested eschatologically. The confession of Jesus Christ as Lord is here also not solely or primarily intended in a ecclesiastical sense, but rather in its cosmic eschatological sense ("that at the name of Jesus every knee should bend, of things in heaven and things on earth, and things under the earth").[17] There is no indication that the name *Kyrios*, as Bousset wishes to demonstrate, refers to the pneumatic Christ, in contrast to the eschatological Christ. Philippians 2:9-11 does not contain materially anything different from Matthew 28:18-20, i.e., the description of the glorification of the Son of Man.

And what we have said not only is true of Philippians 2:11. The proximity of meaning for Paul of the name *Kyrios* with that of the 'Son of Man' is proven by such passages where the parousia of the *Kyrios* is expressly spoken of (1 Thess. 2:19; 3:13; 4:15; 5:23; 2 Thess. 2:1, 8), and where also the eschatological, not cultic, nearness of the *Kyrios* is mentioned (Phil. 4:5), as well as the heavens as the place from where we can expect the second coming of the Lord (Phil. 3:20), and of the revelation of our *Kyrios* of heaven with the angels of his power.[18]

Naturally, all this does not deny that it was of special significance that the *Kurios* name which came to be used of

Christ in this sense, was the same as that which was used in
Hellenistic heathendom for its cultus gods and for its
Caesars.[19] It is very probable that in 1 Corinthians 8:5, Paul
refers to this: "For though there be so-called gods, whether
in heaven or in earth (as there be gods many and lords
many) but to us there is but one God, the Father, of whom
are all things, and we in him; and one Lord Jesus Christ." The
confession of Christ as the Lord thereby acquires in the
mouth of the Christian church and Paul's preaching a certain
polemical sound.[20] Nevertheless, it cannot be stated that
the antithesis posited here between 'the one Lord Jesus
Christ' and the 'many Lords,' clearly gives rise to the origin
of the *Kyrios* title.[21] One can with more justice defend the
position that if the title and confession of Jesus as Lord was
not of a different origin, if it did not have its own root of
existence, the analogy with the pagan religions would have
hindered rather than furthered the use of this title.

Finally, with regard to the pneumatic conception of
Paul's preaching and piety, undoubtedly there exists in
Paul's epistles a very close connection between the Spirit,
as the gift to the church, and the *Kyrios Christos*, exalted
in the heavens. The passage frequently cited by Bousset
(2 Cor. 3:17), "The *Kyrios* is now the spirit," is proof of
this. The question is, however, what is the nature of the
connection. Is this conception of *Kyrios* determined and
produced by the pneumatic piety in the cults, or does
the gift of the pneuma find its explanation and character
in the eschatological *Kyrios*? It cannot be denied, at least
with respect to the basic structure of Paul's preaching, that
the latter is the case. The pneuma is the gift, which flows
out of Christ's eschatological redemptive works; it is the
Spirit of Christ (Rom. 8:10), the spirit of him who has raised
Christ from the dead (vs. 11). The Spirit is 'the first gift'
in which is revealed the definitive redemption which began
with Christ's coming (Rom. 8:23). He is the guarantee of all

that which God will send in Christ (2 Cor. 1:22; 5:5; Eph. 1:14). Especially these latter qualifications (ἀπαρχή and ἀρραβών) established the meaning which the Holy Spirit has in Paul's preaching, and the relationship between the *Kyrios* and *pneuma*. They describe the Spirit as the provisional gift, which in the midst of all the remaining misery (Rom. 8:19ff; 2 Cor. 5:4), is a proof and guarantee of the ultimate redemption in Christ. Therefore, the Spirit in Ephesians 1:14 can also be called 'the guarantee of our inheritance.' He is the one who as such, as the provisional first gift, sealed the believers to this final redemption (2 Cor. 1:22; Eph. 1:13; 4:30). When then in 2 Corinthians 3:17, it is stated that the *Kyrios* is the Spirit, this does not signify that the *Kyrios* is determined completely and entirely by the idea of *pneuma*, but as it clearly appears from the context,[22] the Spirit is the gift of Christ, who already in this era, gives the faithful the freedom to live according to the New Covenant, which gift could not be provided by the law (Cf. Gal. 3:21).[23] Christ, the Lord, is not identical with the Holy Spirit but as the risen Lord and the future redeemer he bestows the Holy Spirit (Cf. Rev. 22:17).

From all this it clearly appears how Paul, on the one hand, repeatedly can ascribe the same gifts and operations respectively to Christ and to the Spirit, and how, nevertheless, on the other hand, everything which Paul says about the Spirit is in keeping with the same redemptive historical consciousness, in which he calls Christ the Lord. The basic idea of Paul's doctrine of the Holy Spirit is not to be sought in a mystical cultus sphere, but in the eschatological sphere.[24] The Spirit is the representative gift of the *Kyrios* during the interim between Christ's resurrection and parousia. The Spirit groans and strives for the time, in which as such he will become superfluous (Rom. 8:23ff; cf. 1 Cor. 13:8ff). There is no support in anything which Paul says about the nature and operation of the Spirit for the notion that Paul transformed the original Palestinian Christian expectation

of the end into a Hellenistic Christianity. Rather the opposite is the case. The statements about the pneuma cause
us to see that in Paul the redemptive historical *post* is not
transformed into a timeless *trans,* but that the pneumatic
is subordinated in his preaching to the recognition and
expectation of Christ as the exalted and future *Kyrios.*

Finally it is also evident that Paul's preaching of Christ
as the *Kyrios* and as the *pneuma* stands in a clear and unbreakable unity with the faith and confession of the early
church. That which Peter proclaimed in his sermon at
Pentecost of the *Kyrios*-nature of Christ, of the Spirit as the
gift of the final period, and of Christ as the recipient and
source of this gift (Acts 2:17, 33), also forms the heart of
Paul's *kerygma* concerning the *Kyrios,* and the Spirit. Therefore, there is in this respect no cleft between what Jesus proclaimed of himself and that which Paul proclaimed of Christ.
Everything finds its place within the framework of fulfillment, the foundation of which is found in Jesus' preaching
of the kingdom, and the mystery and content of which is
found in the person of Christ himself. Paul, as the early
church at Jerusalem, simply represents within this fulfillment a more advanced stage, qualified by Christ's resurrection. No doubt, the content of Paul's preaching, in this
respect too, comes to a fuller expression than that of the
first church. One can also observe how the tremendous
richness of the redemption already revealed in Christ, sometimes placed the provisional element in the background. On
the other hand, the very passages which in the epistles speak
of the *pneuma* bring the element of expectation and of longing
to the foreground. In all this diversity there exists, however,
a powerful unity, not only in Paul's own preaching, but also
between Paul and the early church, and between Paul and
Jesus. It is the reality of the kingdom proclaimed by Jesus
which reveals itself here in Christ as the exalted *Messiah-
Kyrios* and in his Spirit as the gift by which the heavenly

Father enables his children to live on the earth, and which leads them into the light of the great day of salvation (Luke 11:13; John 14:15, 16).[25]

17. The Son of God

No less radical than the preceding is the affirmation that the person of Jesus had for the Palestinian Christendom—in conformity with Jesus' self-revelation—only the significance of a man, but that Paul, under the influence of the Hellenistic community, transformed the person of Jesus into a divine being. This transition from the early Christian to the Hellenistic *kerygma* is said to be seen very clearly in the different usage of the title applied to Christ: *the Son of God*. The early Christian church also called Christ by this name. But whereas it thereby only meant to indicate Jesus' messianic kingship, without ascribing any ontological associations to this title, for the pagan hearers it was self-evident that the title referred to the divine being, the divine nature of Christ, because of which he was distinguished from the human sphere. This ontological conception of Christ's sonship is current in the relevant Pauline passages and in contrast to Palestinian Christianity, placed Paul in principle on the side of Hellenistic Christendom.[26] This construction forms one of the most central components of the problem 'Jesus and Paul.' It concerns the historical legitimacy of the Pauline *kerygma* and the entire faith of the Christian church, in their very heart and center, and therefore, warrants an extensive discussion.

It would, however, be a mistake to believe that Bultmann, and others are satisfied with the explanation of the title 'Son of God' in terms of these two *religionsgeschichtliche* 'types' (the Jewish-Christian official messianic name and the Hellenistic Christian essential-name). In the first place the name 'Son of God,' which repeatedly occurs in the synoptic gospels (concerning which we will have more to say later), is thought to represent still another Hellenistic type. It is not so much his divine essence or his pre-existence which marks Jesus as the Son of God, but rather his mysterious miraculous power. According to Bultmann, and others, the synoptic gospels, insofar as they describe Jesus as the Son of God, do so according to the pattern of the $\theta\epsilon\hat{\iota}o\iota$ $\check{\alpha}\nu\delta\rho\epsilon\varsigma$, well-known in Hellenism, who begotten by the deity, and by their heroic deeds, spiritual accomplishments, or as benefactors of humanity, appear to be more than ordinary people. These also have claimed to be Sons of God, $\upsilon\iotao\grave{\iota}$ $\theta\epsilono\hat{\upsilon}$ and were recognized as such. In this sense is to be explained the synoptic account that Jesus was 'adopted' as the Son of God by the Spirit, sent at his baptism. Related to this is also the idea appearing in Matthew and Luke of Jesus being conceived by the Holy Ghost (Matt. 1:20), or by the power of the Almighty (Luke 1:35), a notion current not only in the Greek tradition, but also in the Babylonian, and especially in the Egyptian dynasty legends and which was assimilated into the gospels from the Jewish Hellenism in Egypt. This conception of Jesus' divine sonship, it is said, was later engulfed by the Hellenistic conception of the type encountered in Paul and John, according to which Jesus is the pre-existent Son of God who became man. And this second notion was then united to a third type of figure of the Son of God; i.e., that of the cosmic Son of God, derived from the gnostic myth.[27]

Before examining the source material on the basis of which this conception is defended, we shall indicate certain historical objections which make it extremely improbable that Paul, under the influence of Greek thought, transformed a human official title so that it acquired a divine, ontological significance.

In the first place, Paul, in spite of his travel among the heathen, remained a Jew in his heart and soul. It is inconceivable that he could accept without protest a view of the divine nature of Christ which originated in heathendom, when to do so would mean a material adaptation of polytheism which he himself despised.[28] And it would also signify a complete break with the early Christian preaching of Jesus Christ with which he considered his own to be in complete harmony. It is difficult to conceive how all this can be harmonized in the above-sketched 'development' of the New Testament Christology.

Secondly, that such a revolution in the deepest foundations of Christianity could take place—not in the course of centuries but—in the first ten or twenty years of Christianity in a completely silent manner, is historically unexplainable. Nothing is known of any opposition between Paul (the Hellenistic churches) and the other apostles on this point. Here also it ought to be remembered what could be established in the preceding[29] concerning Paul's relationship to heathendom and to the apostolic tradition. This reconstruction of the development of early Christendom confronts us with unsolvable riddles. For even if one can conceive that after the resurrection Paul and the leaders of the church at Jerusalem were submerged in a flood of pagan conceptions, nothing in the New Testament indicates that they forgot the distinction between what was revealed in Christ and the polytheistic conceptions of the surrounding pagan world. The very opposite is easily proven.

In the third place, Lagrange in particular has pointed out[30] that while in the Hellenistic pagan world, the faith in the sons of gods was universal and that a divine life and nature was ascribed to them in various ways, nevertheless, such sonship always has its demonstrable beginning, e.g., in the intercourse of the gods among themselves or with mankind. But when Paul calls Jesus Christ the Son of God he means something entirely different. For Paul always bases his conception upon the pre-existence of Christ. Christ's human nature had a beginning but his being-the-Son-of God did not, as is clear from the statements concerning Christ's pre-existence already discussed.[31]   There is, therefore, a great cleft between Paul's faith in Jesus as the Son of God and the *apotheoses* of his time.   Lagrange correctly asks how Paul could have derived such a notion from the pagans when the latter did not have any idea of it?   It is true that Bultmann would not explain Paul's view of the deity of Christ in terms of the general faith of the people, but in terms of the gnostic myth.[32]   But therefore his assumption that the title 'Son of God,' as used by Paul and as it appears in the Hel-lenistic church, was self-evident to pagan listeners, is very debatable.[33]   For no one can affirm that this gnostic myth, even if it already existed at the time of Paul, was generally current among those whom Paul tried to bring to the faith in Christ.

   These objections are of a general nature.   But the New Testament material to which an appeal is made for this con-struction also clearly points in another direction.   From a closer examination of the available data it ought to be crystal clear that things in the New Testament are in any case much more complicated than the *religionsgeschichtliche* school would have us believe.

   As for the Acts, one must admit, at first sight there is nothing of the unmistakable clarity with which Paul speaks of the essential relation between Christ as the Son, and the Father.   One could hold that comparative material, in the strict sense of the word, is nearly lacking, because the title 'Son of God' appears only once in the first half of the book of Acts, in the statement that Paul, after his conversion, "straightway preached in the synagogue that Jesus is the Son of God" (Acts 9:20).   And from this single reference it cannot be determined with sufficient certainty how the title 'the Son of God' must here be understood. If the question is viewed, however, in a broader sense, an essential unity or likeness between Christ and the Father is not spoken of in Acts, in the explicit sense of Paul (and John). This does not in any sense imply that the faith and preaching of the early church, with respect to the person of Christ, can be explained within the framework of a then current human[34] conception of the Messiah. Rather it ought to be established that nowhere in the entire New Testament *kerygma,* including the book of Acts, can a stage be distinguished in which an absolute divine meaning is not ascribed to the work and also to the person of Jesus as the Christ.

Already on the day of Pentecost, Peter proclaimed Jesus as the Christ, whose resurrection was foretold by David; who was not only David's son, but also his Lord, exalted by God, and from whom in the heavens proceeded the gift of the eschatological, redemptive period, the Holy Spirit, and to whom, as the one now sitting on the right hand of God's throne, is now given as Lord and Christ, the power and judgment over his enemies (Acts 2:29-35). In the later pronouncements of Acts, all this is confirmed. This glorification of Christ is more than can be ascribed to any creature; it consists in the control over God's own power in heaven and on earth, in being the judge over the living and the dead, and in giving of forgiveness of sins through his name (Acts 10:42-43). Of the name of Christ we read in Acts, not only that it works healing (Acts 3:6; 4:10), but also that it is the object of faith (3:16), of preaching (9:15, cf. vs. 27), of supplication in prayer (7:59; 9:14, 21). It is the only name under heaven through which salvation is possible (4:12); it has absolute significance, without any reserve or qualification, as the name that is worthy of suffering and of the worship of the saints (Acts 5:41; 9:21). From the last passage it appears that the person of Christ had an absolute significance in the early Christian church. For what is applicable to the name of Jahwe in the Old Testament is here also valid of the name of Jesus.[35]　And that we find these expressions directly in Acts points to the fact that immediately after the resurrection, divine honor and quality was ascribed to Jesus as the risen exalted Christ.[36]　All this is included in such Christological titles as the 'Saviour,' chapter 5:31; 13:23, and the 'Lord,' 1:6; 2:36; 7:59; 9:1, 5, etc. Of a special significance here is the continuous use of the name 'Lord.' It describes the exalted risen Christ with the same word which is used in the Septuagint to translate 'Jahwe.' From here, the description of Christ as Lord receives an increasingly pregnant significance as a divine name of glory.[37]

To answer the question of the origin of this faith, one must certainly point to the resurrection.　Also in the gospel of John, the confession of Thomas that Jesus is 'Lord and God' occurred after the resurrection (John 20:28).　The resurrection was for the apostles in the early church not only the proof that Jesus was the Messiah, but that he was the Messiah in an unknown, divine sense, which transcended all conceptions previously held of the Messiah.　Braun correctly writes: "The message of the Apostles of the resurrected Christ contains a complete Christology."[38]　In the genuineness of Christ's resurrection from the dead lies one of the main sources of the faith that Jesus Christ participates in the divine glory and majesty; for he did not rise again to re-enter earthly life, but to disclose himself to his own from the heavens.　Apart from the resurrection, New Testament Christology is inexplicable.　But given the truth of the resurrection, this Christology is consistent and natural,[39] and it becomes clear how in many messianic titles, ascribed to Jesus, and pronouncements spoken of him, the messianic and the divine go together.　In the resurrection of Christ which elevates him to the glory of God, the church came to understand that he, whom they had known as Jesus of Nazareth, belonged to another world than to the one in which he was born; that he not only in his end or goal, but also in his origin and existence was determined by this divine glory as it appeared in his resurrection. Therefore, the presupposition which Bultmann apparently accepts, that within the early church, the name 'Son of God' merely indicates Jesus' messianic kingship,[40] whereas, in Paul the ontic character of this sonship clearly appears, is a schematization that does not represent the actual state of affairs. In Paul, that the official kingship is also intended in his description of Christ as the Son of God, is undeniable (Cf. e.g., Rom. 1:3). It is equally evident that according to Acts, the absolute divine significance ascribed to Jesus Christ in the early church, not only is related to his work and office but also to his person. Such is not yet a formulation of the doctrine of the person and essence of Christ; it is not a theology but simply the believing confession and witness of the church concerning Christ. But the content of this confession was from the very beginning illuminated and determined by the resurrection, in its supernatural and divine character.

We must go deeper, however, and return to Jesus' self-revelation during his life on the earth. *Behind the entire New Testament kerygma of Jesus as the supernatural Son of God, lies as the actual and final explanation, the basic factum of the self-revelation of Jesus' super-human, absolute person, as presented to us in the Gospels.* That this is true of the gospel of John needs no further argument. But it is also valid of the synoptic gospels, even though on the basis of all sorts of classifications of the sources (an earlier practice) and *formgeschichtliche* manipulations currently popular, it is still thought that a purely human conception of the person of Jesus can be found here.

Already the general picture which the synoptic gospels provide of Jesus' earthly life is not only determined by his entry and participation in human life, by being born of a

woman, by his birth, suffering, and death, but it is no less
determined by his superhuman and divine glory, which in
spite of its temporary concealment could not remain hidden.
Light is thrown upon the latter by Jesus' miracles, the authority in his speaking and his commanding, and from the supernatural, 'surprising' and 'startling' impression which he made
upon everyone.[41] It also appears from the name: 'The Son
of Man' by which Jesus preferred to qualify his messianic
mission and by which he not only indicated his poverty,
humiliation, and the suffering and death placed upon him
by God, but—in a profound twofold unity—also indicated the
transcendent character of his person and work. This name
reflects that which was said in Daniel's vision of the apocalyptic figure to whom all power was given by the Ancient
of Days, as it appears, not only from Jesus' word before the
Sanhedrin, but also in other passages of the gospel, in a
nearly literal relation to the words of Daniel 7, Matthew
28:18 (Cf. also 9:6, etc.). Also the discussion with Pharisees
over the theme, 'David's Son,' and 'David's Lord' (Matt.
22:41-46), clearly refers to this transcendent glorification of
the Messiah. He is the Son of David, but at the same time
his Lord; he is the One who according to Psalm 110 will
be exalted by God to his right hand. In the gospels this
unmistakably points to Christ's future divine glory. And it
is also in this sense that Jesus calls himself the Son to whom
the Father has given all things (Matt. 11:27).

    We hereby touch upon the very comprehensive and im-
portant question as to what significance must be ascribed in
the synoptic gospels to the title, the 'Son of God.' The question
is of such great importance because this name in the gospels
not only appears in a single instance—as in the first chapters
of the book of Acts—but it constitutes one of the most essential components of what the synoptic gospels disclose of the
significance of Jesus' person and work. It is the name by
which Jesus was announced by the angel to Mary (Luke

1:35, Cf. vs. 32), whereby he was made known by God himself, first at his baptism (Mark 1:11), and later during his exaltation on the mountain (Mark 9:7). As the Son of God, he was tempted by the devil in the wilderness (Matt. 4:3, 6), spoken to by the demons (Mark 3:11; 5:7), confessed by Peter (Mark 8:16), and called into account by the high priest (Mark 14:64), mocked on the cross (Matt. 27:40-43), and confessed by the Centurion (Mark 15:39). As the Son, Jesus speaks of himself in an absolute manner at the end of his apocalyptic speech (Mark 13:32), in the commandment of baptism (Matt. 28:19), and very particularly in the well-known statement in Matthew 11:27, Luke 10:22: "No man knoweth who the Son is, but the Father, and who the Father is, but the Son, and he to whom the Son will reveal him." In addition there are other passages to be cited in which Jesus speaks of God as of his Father, as, for example, in Matthew 7:21; 10:32ff; 12:50ff; 15:13; 16:27; 18:10, 19; 20:23; 25:34; 26:29, 39, 53, and others. From these statements, which can be multiplied,[42] it appears how important is the significance which must be ascribed to the title 'The Son of God' in the synoptic gospels.

It is clear that with this name the significance of Jesus' person is described in a very exclusive manner, and that the old liberal conception, which basically thought that nothing else was expressed than that all men are children of God, falls far short of the truth.[43]

The affirmation of Bultmann, and others, that the synoptic description of Jesus as the Son of God followed the pattern of the god-men ($\theta\epsilon\hat{\iota}o\iota$ $\check{\alpha}\nu\delta\rho\epsilon\varsigma$) known to Hellenism, not only touches the very heart of the historical trustworthiness of the synoptic gospels, but, as has been demonstrated extensively by J. Bieneck,[44] is entirely in conflict with the character of the divine sonship ascribed to Jesus in the synoptic gospels. In polytheistic Hellenism, the boundaries between the divine and the human are eradicated in numerous ways and the divine predicate is, therefore ascribed very royally to every unusual human, whether a prophet, a philosopher, or a worker of wonders (Simon Magnus and Apollonius of Tyana are outstanding examples) and even to the Roman Caesars. In the synoptic gospels, in contrast, the name, the 'Son of God' refers to the absolutely exclusive relation between Jesus Christ and the only true God. And no matter how much one can mention various characteristics, in the life of the 'god-men,' which at first glance show a similarity to what is told of Jesus (e.g., possession of supernatural gifts, power over the elements, sovereign control over fellowmen, appearance as a peacemaker, helper and friend of the oppressed and the poor; miraculous events accompanying birth and death), such are not basically different from the sagas and fairy tales of all nations in all periods, and certainly such do not produce a typical 'schema' for the life of Jesus. And what says even much more, whereas the divinity of these θεῖοι ἄνδρες is deduced from the particular gifts and powers ascribed to them, the sonship of Christ, according to the synoptic gospels, lies on an entirely different niveau and bears an entirely different character. Only in a single instance is it brought into direct contact with Jesus' wonders (Matt. 14:33). Mostly it stands, however, in the closest relation with the entirely unique significance of Christ's commission by the Father; thus, for example, at his baptism, his transfiguration, the confession of Peter, the question of the high priest. The concern in the first place is not with Jesus' miraculous power but with the divine authority with which his person is endowed in everything which he does, says, and suffers. On the other hand, as the Son of God, Jesus, unlike the Hellenistic miracle workers, does not appear in self-exaltation and self-conceit, as a despot.[45] But, as the Son, Jesus is subject in all things to the Father, and in obedient sacrifice gives himself to the will of the Father. Jesus, the eschatological Saviour, accomplishes the divine task given to him as the fulfiller of the law and the prophets. Such is incomparably disclosed in the devil's appeal to his sonship in the wilderness, and Jesus' wrestling in prayer in order to accomplish the will of the Father in Gethsemane. If the background, the 'eschatological setting,' in which the entire work of Christ, as the Son of God functions, is kept in mind, there can then be no question of an essential agreement between Christ and the bizarre miracle workers of Hellenism, and one is then simply amazed at the ease and arbitrariness with which these completely dissimilar entities are related to each other. And we have not even mentioned the incredible assumption that the early Christian church supposedly described a posteriori the earthly life of Christ and the risen and exalted Lord, in terms of a pagan miracle worker, a doubtful figure in every respect!

The positive significance of the name, 'Son of God,' is, however, not yet sufficiently described. A question of special importance is whether the exclusiveness of this title had a relationship only to Jesus' messianic authenticity or whether in the synoptic gospels, it also points to a deeper ontological characterization of Christ's person. The view that the Son of God, in the older Christian texts, simply is a 'synonym' for 'Messiah,' has frequently found supporters.[46] Others are of the opinion, however, that this name must be sharply distinguished from the messianic titles and that it—and not the messianic titles—brought to expression that the revelation of Christ is concerned with something that far exceeds all human hopes, thoughts, and expectations.[47] In our opinion, without further qualification, the name 'Son of God' does not simply express an ontological relationship between Jesus and the Father. It can also be understood as an official messianic title, and in the synoptic gospels, at least in various passages, it must be so understood, e.g., when in Luke 3:22,[48] the voice from heaven applies to Jesus the Old Testament phrase of Psalm 2:7. And likewise, in Luke 4:41, when the

798

devils cry, "Thou art Christ the Son of God," this is to be
explained clearly as a reference to the Messiah.[49]   Also elsewhere the title the 'Son of God' is apparently intended to
be used as an expression equivalent to the 'Messiah' (Cf.
Matt. 16:16, "Thou art the Christ, the Son of the Living God"
and vs. 20, "then charged he his disciples that they should
tell no man that he was Jesus the Christ"). It is also to be
noted that where the one evangelist speaks of the Son of
God, the others or one of them speaks of 'the Christ' or of
the 'Christ of God' (Cf. Matt. 16:16 with Mark 8:29, and
Luke 9:20; also cf. Matt. 26:63, and Mark 14:61, with Luke
22:67).[50]

On the basis of these passages,[51] it is not to be denied
that the title the 'Son of God' in the synoptic gospels is most
often intended to be a more exact description of Christ's
messianic authenticity.   But this does not deny that this
name at the same time is pregnant with a deeper, divine
meaning.   In our opinion the term, as a description of the
Messiah, originally does not indicate an ontological but an
official relationship between God and the messianic king.
And in the gospels, especially when used by ordinary men,[52]
it is most frequently employed in this sense.   But the fact
remains, nevertheless, that when the term 'the Son of God'
is used in the revelation of Jesus as the Christ, by the Father
and by Jesus himself, it acquires a much more inclusive content, although—in keeping with the entire character of this
revelation—such was not immediately made explicit in all
its consequences.   For an interpretation which exclusively
works with preconceived *religionsgeschichtliche* schemata
(whether derived from the Old Testament, later Judaism,
or the Greek world) such a view as ours may be unacceptable, but when Jesus' self-revelation is accepted in its own
real independence, as a result of the glory of his divine
person, the necessity of such an explanation disappears, and
the integrity of the synoptic tradition does not need to be

doubted. In his self-revelation, in many respects, Jesus employs the categories of the Old Testament expectation, in which the official glory of the Messiah and not the ontical comes to the fore. *All this acquires an unsuspected supernatural content only in the fulfillment.* It then appears that all the stages along which the stream of the revelation previously was led, could not contain the pleroma of fulfillment. When a gradually richer Christological terminology occurs in the New Testament than in the Old Testament, or also when the Old Testament names and symbols acquire a more inclusive content in the New Testament, such is, therefore, not due to an influx of Hellenistic mythology into the early church, but to the fact that the reality of the fulfillment, sent in Christ, can no longer find an adequate expression in the terms and 'schemata' of expectation.

Such is clearly the case with reference to the title 'the Son of God' in the synoptic tradition. Undoubtedly, when used in Israel of the messianic king, the title, 'the Son of God,' originally was an official predicate and not an ontological description. Nevertheless, in the synoptic gospels it clearly acquires an additional connotation. In this manner is to be explained the frequent usage of the title in the gospels which cannot be explained in terms of its usage as a messianic title. In the Old Testament and later Judaism it very seldom appears as such.[53] The frequency of the title in the gospels is an indication of the special grandeur of the messianic Jesus. That this majesty of the Messiah, as the Son of God, is more than can be expressed in terms of an office, appears the clearest from the way in which Jesus speaks of himself in the absolute sense as of 'the Son' (Mark 13:32; Matt. 21:37). The depth of this expression comes unmistakably to light in the well-known passages in Matthew 11:27 and Luke 10:22, which speak not only of the absolute power of the Son ("all things are delivered unto me of my father"), but the knowledge of the Son is also called a mys-

tery equal to that of the Father ("and no man knoweth the
Son, but the Father; neither knoweth any man the Father
save the Son, and he to whomsoever the Son will reveal
Him"). It is in our opinion indisputable that in this self-
revelation of Jesus, as the Son, (Cf. also Matt. 28:19), the
sonship of Christ implies more than messiahship. And
on this basis alone can the proper tenor of the entire synoptic
kerygma concerning Jesus, as the Son of God, be established.
One cannot say that the synoptic gospels explicitly teach
with so many words the eternal sonship of Christ. Nevertheless, the glorification of Jesus' sonship cannot be expressed
in terms of the categories of office. There is a deeper relationship, a deeper unity between Christ and the Father.
Especially the words in which the Father himself speaks
of Jesus as 'My Son,' and 'My Beloved Son' (at his baptism
and his transfiguration) must so be understood.[55] Even
though their primary meaning is messianic, in the light of
Jesus' progressive self-revelation these words contain a
deeper mystery than that of a messiah in the possession of
superhuman power, as is indicated by Matthew from the
very beginning by the expression *God-with-us,* in the *essential,* ontical sense of the word (Matt. 1:23).

There is, therefore, basically no difference between the
account of the synoptics and that of John concerning Jesus'
self-revelation. Undoubtedly, the gospel of John speaks,
at least for later hearers, more clearly and frankly than the
synoptic gospels of Jesus' pre-existence,[56] his divine sonship,
and his unity with the Father. The prologue to John's
gospel, which explicitly identifies the Logos with God, indicates how the gospel ought to be read and how Jesus' words
ought to be understood, as since the resurrection, the disciples
confessed (by the mouth of Thomas) Jesus as Lord and God
(John 20:28). No matter how noteworthy it may be that
all this appears in John; and no matter how the style and
composition of the gospel, especially its argumentation,

sometimes appears to erase the boundary between the writing of history and *kerygma*, the fact remains, nevertheless, that it is just John who lays all emphasis upon the *historical*, *visible*, and *tangible* character of Jesus' divine self-revelation (John 1:14, 18; John 19:35; 20:24; 1 John 1:1ff). While a distinction is therefore made in the modality between Jesus' self-revelation in John and in the synoptic gospels, in the sense that the former is a more explicit description of his pre-existence and of his unique ontological relation to the Father, such does not need to be explained in terms of the further developed kerygmatic character of the fourth gospel. Rather, to do justice to the fourth gospel the fact must be ascertained that the eye-witness character of the author in this gospel receives more emphasis and indirectly—in all sorts of exact references to time and other precise historical characteristics—appears more clearly in the foreground, than in the witness of the synoptics. And in the form in which it has been delivered to us, John's gospel bears a much more personal character. Therefore, in the gospel of John, the original impression which the person of Jesus Christ made upon his direct environment appears to be retained in its purest and clearest form. Unless the fourth gospel is in this latter respect considered to be the greatest falsification, its exalted Christological statements must be taken as a proof that the author, as an eye-witness and intimate associate of Jesus, was close to the sources where the entire stream of the New Testament *kerygma* originated. And it therefore follows that not only in the resurrection, but also in the personal intercourse of his disciples with Jesus, the origin of the faith of the church lies in his superhuman glory and divine mode of existence. The actual mystery of the passages which bear upon Christ's divine being must then not be sought in the *Umwelt* (environment), but in the person of Jesus himself, or as John says, *"and we have beheld his glory, the glory as of the only begotten of the Father, full of*

grace and truth" (John 1:14), and elsewhere "that which was
from the beginning, which we have heard, and which we
have seen with our eyes, which we have looked upon, and
our hands have handled, of the word of life . . . declare we
unto you" (1 John 1:1ff).

In view of our discussion thus far one cannot find in Paul
a decisive transition in the New Testament *kerygma*, in the
sense that a human and official conception of the Son of
God is replaced by an ontical conception. Although Paul,
even as John and the later writers of the New Testament,
also gives a more expressed and explicit view of the deity
of Christ, it is not to be denied that the person of Christ,
in the entire New Testament *kerygma*, bears a superhuman
and supernatural character. There can be no question of a
speculative or *religionsgeschichtliche* development. The
power of the revelation of Jesus Christ before his death, and
after his resurrection, and in his appearance to the other
apostles, and to Paul is everywhere evident and operative.
What Paul proclaims of Jesus Christ as the Son of God
rests upon nothing else and is not different from what was
revealed to the apostles before him. Such a position does
not imply that from the beginning there was in the Christian
church a precisely formulated dogma of the person of Christ.
There was rather a gradual and broader awareness, in the
faith of the eyewitnesses and of the church, that God himself
had come to them in Christ. Because the faith of the church,
and the *kerygma* included within it, did not directly receive
its full expansion, does not at all imply that the confession
of Christ as the true and essential Son of God, is the fruit
of an immanent development. This confession was rather
the fruit and revelation of the incarnate exalted Son of
God, of which the implications, independently of all *religionsgeschichtliche* influences, are brought to ever clearer expression in the confession and *kerygma*. As with respect to the
name *Kyrios*, so also with respect to the divine sonship of

Christ, there is nothing to hinder us from understanding and explaining the Pauline *kerygma* in terms of the revelation he had received, and in terms of the spiritual unity of Paul's message, with the Palestinian church and with Jesus' own self-revelation.

18. The Descended Redeemer

Closely connected with the preceding, but of a much broader scope, is a third point advanced as proof of the pagan Hellenistic influence in Paul's Christology. The argument in question is not only related to specific predicates ascribed to the person of Christ, but also to the entire Pauline conception of Christ's redemptive work. The latter is thought to betray, in many respects, the influence of the so-called gnostic myth of the 'redeemed Redeemer.' The Pauline view of redemption is therefore to be distinguished in a decisive manner from the original messianic view of Christ, found in the early Palestinian church.

This gnostic interpretation of Paul's Christology is still relatively recent. And we have seen[57] it has to a large extent superseded the *religionsgeschichtliche* interpretation in terms of the Hellenistic mystery-myths. Its most prominent representative is Bultmann.[58] Bultmann affirms that in the faith of the early Palestinian church, Jesus was still the 'Man' exalted by God (the Son of Man), whose quick return was eagerly expected and to whom the significance of the future world judge was ascribed. Gradually, but in a relatively short time, a much more inclusive interpretation of Christ's person and work was formed which then dominated the church, and which gave to the Christian faith the character of a totalitarian *redemptive* religion, in the full sense of the word. The significance of Jesus' person and work was then interpreted with the concepts of the gnostic redemptive myth. Christ now became the divine figure which preceded from

the heavenly world of light, the Son of the Most High, sent
into the world by the Father, and who hidden in human
form, brought redemption through his work. This myth is
thought to be clearly evident in Paul, especially in his
Christuslied of Philippians 2:6-11, in which Christ is spoken
of as the pre-existent divine being who abandoned the
heavenly regions, and appeared in the form of a servant,
and who after his death was exalted to be the Lord. This
myth is also behind the pregnant definitions of Paul in
1 Corinthians 2:8ff, concerning the mysterious divine wisdom, which the 'princes of this world' did not know, since
otherwise they would not have crucified the Lord of Glory.
These powers, in conformity with the gnostic myths, did
not recognize the divine being who descended from heaven
in his garb as a man, so that by crucifying him they brought
destruction to themselves. In this sense is to be understood[59]
such passages as 2 Corinthians 8:9 ("though he was rich,
yet for your sakes he became poor"); Ephesians 4:8-10 (the
descent of Christ to "the lower parts of the earth," and his
ascent again from these regions); and 1 Timothy 3:16 ("God
was manifested in the flesh, justified in the spirit, seen of
angels, preached unto the Gentiles . . . received up in His
glory.") In all this Christ acquires the significance of a
cosmic figure, who descended into this world to conduct
the struggle against the dark powers which threatened man
in his deepest being; and behind this, as the real origin of
this myth, lays the gnostic 'Selbst-und Welt-verständnis'
(understanding of one's self and of the world), with which
Christendom displays a deep kinship, and which can be
expressed as the consciousness of the principal difference of
all human-being from all worldly being.[60]

In this Bultmann finds a transition to the modern feeling of life, for example, as this comes to expression in the
new existential philosophy.

Before we examine the material content of this interpretation of Paul's Christology in more detail, we ought first to notice the very uncertain historical foundation upon which it rests. The sources available for our knowledge of the gnostic myth, at least with respect to the Mandean, Hermetic, and Manichean writings are of a much later date, and part of them, at least appear centuries after the writing of the New Testament, and, in the form in which they are preserved, are clearly dependent, at least in part, upon Christendom. Manicheanism is without qualification a post-Christian syncretistic phenomenon. And with respect to the age of the Mandean books, cited in this connection, it is certain that the editorship by which these writings have come to us, is very late (about the year 700).[61] It is, however, at present believed by many that the gnosis, which forms the basic tendency of the Mandean religion, is a pre-Christian phenomenon. The question is, however, how far is this also true of the religious conceptions in this literature, appealed to as the origin of the Pauline Christology, i.e., to what one calls the myth of the 'redeemed Redeemer.'

The boldest hypothesis which has been in vogue for awhile is that the Mandean sect (which we now know as a small religious community in south Irak) had lived before the coming of Christ in the neighborhood of Palestine and that John the Baptist, who appears in the Mandean literature, can be explained in terms of this sect. Thus, it is thought that there was a direct influence of this sect upon the original Christianity. The circle of John, out of which Jesus also came forth, would thus be the nursery of a very early gnosis, which freely mixed Babylonian, Persian, and Syrian elements with basic Jewish ideas, grouped around the old Iranian myth of the primal man who descended from the heavens. It is here that the origin of the New Testament Christology is thought to lie. This conception advanced by the translator of the principal Mandean text, M. Lidzbardski, and others, appears too fantastic, and has been refuted for example, by Lietzmann. The latter writes: "This interpretation is very ensnaring and it offers unthought of perspectives for a new understanding of early Christendom, yet we must renounce it without delay."[62] It is established that the sections of this literature in which John the Baptist is spoken of belong to the latest 'parts' and originate, at the very earliest, in the seventh century.

There is thus no proof of any direct influence of the Mandean gnosis upon the early Palestinian Christianity.[63] The question remains whether there is a sufficient basis to assume that the myth of the 'redeemed Redeemer' actually proceeded the origin of Christendom and can in any way have had an influence upon Paul's Christological conception. Bultmann, and his school, display a very great degree of freedom in ascertaining genetic connections, which would make Paul dependent upon a gnostic doctrine of redemption. Others, however, who are no less informed in these matters, point to the shaky historical foundation of this construction. Thus, especially, E. Percy in an extensive investigation concludes that the gnostic idea of redemption, as it appears in the Mandean literature, can more easily be explained in terms of Christendom than vice versa. Percy demonstrates that except for the Mandean and the Hermetic literature, the figure of the gnostic redeemer rests in any case upon a syncreticism with the Christian conception of the Redeemer, e.g., the Manichean literature. And where in the Mandean writings a redeemer is spoken of who descended from the heavens and who appeared in *human history*, Christian influence is here unmistakable. In other parts of the same writings, which do not display any Christian influence, there is also mention of the descent of the Son of God. But the redeemer is then a *pre-historical*, mythological, hero-figure, who carries on a struggle with all sorts of dark primeval powers, but who is not set forth as a redeemer. According to Percy, this indicates that the gnostic idea of a redeemer in the Mandean writings must be interpreted in terms of the Christian notion and not in the reverse fashion.[64] Percy will not accept anything of the thesis of Reitzenstein[65] that in this Mandean literature we have to do with a so-called Iranian mystery of redemption, according to which the Christian idea of redemption (in Paul, for example) can be traced back to Iranian influence. Rather, Percy denies that the mythical figure of Gayomart, who according to Reitzenstein appears in the Iranian text as the bearer of these ideas, is to be viewed as a redeemer. And Percy comes to the far-reaching conclusion that outside of Christianity, and such religious conceptions which have fallen under its influence (as those of the Manicheans), the entire notion of redemption (prearranged from above and realized by the entrance of a heavenly Redeemer), does not appear in the religions of the Near East.[66] Percy's investigation has left its impression; especially the fact that in the Mandean literature out of which the pre-Christian origin of the figure of the 'redeemed Redeemer' is supposedly derived, a redeemer who must share the fate of the souls he came to redeem, only appears in a very few places, and then in such places that stand under Christian influence. Therefore, such an author as Jeremias, on the basis of what Percy has brought to light, rejects the entire conception of Reitzenstein, according to which the Manichean doctrine of the 'redeemed Redeemer' (a divine primeval man, engulfed in matter from which he is saved, and out of which he saves the souls of men, and redeems them from their imprisonment) is of pre-Christian Iranian origin and forms the pattern of a pre-Christian gnostic doctrine of redemption.[67] Whatever the figures of the redeemer may have been in the Persian and pre-Christian gnostic religiosity—according to Jeremias—the doctrine of the 'redeemed Redeemer,' who descended from the heavens to draw to himself or share in the fate of the enslaved souls, as this is known

in later Manicheanism, cannot have been the origin of the
humiliated and exalted Redeemer in the New Testament.
The reverse is rather the case.[68] Against the frontal attack of Percy, Bultmann has tried to defend his theory that
the doctrine of redemption of Paul (and John) ought to be
interpreted in terms of pre-Christian gnosticism. Bultmann
must recognize, however, that only in the gnostic texts which
are clearly under the influence of Christendom does the
redeemer appear as a specifically historical figure. In his
opinion it does not follow that this redeemer figure in the
Mandean literature is based upon a syncretism of Christianity and gnosis. For in the first place the historicity of
the Redeemer in the Mandean text in question is very
vague. Moreover, there is no trace to be discovered of any
likeness or agreement with the historical Jesus (no birth,
no death, no resurrection). Bultmann thinks, therefore,
that this redeemer figure, his 'coming' to man, etc., must be
seen in its unity with the mythological heroes of primeval
times. What this figure in non-specified primal times had
to take upon himself in his struggle with the powers of dark-
ness, is also what souls in time have to conquer in their own
way. There is also a similar parallel between the destiny
of these heroes and what can be ascertained of the souls.
In the language of the cult, etc., these primeval events are
made historical with an application to this struggle of the
souls.[69]

No matter how the latter is conceived, it is obvious
that a closer examniation clearly reveals the weakness of
the basis upon which the post-Christian Manichean doctrine
of the 'redeemed Redeemer' is conceived of as a pre-Christian
gnostic myth. If there is any basis at all for such a pre-
Christian gnostic Redeemer figure, it certainly is not founded
on an historical figure (so as in Mani) but in a mythological
hero from a primeval period. The latter appears in a cosmological myth and 'redemption' consists in the relation

between the fate and struggle of later souls, and the cosmic struggle of a hero from a primeval period (described *per consequentiam* as 'Redeemer'). Even if one does not wish to accept (with such an author as Percy) that there can be no notion of a pre-Christian gnostic redeemer, the Redeemer quality of the figure which must serve here is in any case very vague and unspecified, and can only be established with the help of a very complicated interpretation-technique.

So much for the literary historical aspect of the matter. In our opinion when approached from a material point of view, the situation is still more precarious with respect to the affirmation that this gnostic myth lay at the foundation of the Pauline (and Johannine) doctrine of redemption. To see this it seems sufficient simply to compare the main features of both of these views. One need only think of the following:

1. The redemption in Christ proclaimed by Paul has a clearly demonstrable and datable *historical* character. The gnostic myth speaks of an inconceivable primeval period and has no relation to a single historical figure.

2. The Redeemer whom Paul preaches was born as a man and was a man in the full sense of the word. As such he sojourned among men, suffered, died, and rose again from the dead. The gnostic Redeemer, insofar as he does not show clear 'Christian' characteristics, as in the case of the Manicheans, is a mythical hero from a primeval period, who conducts a cosmic war against unspeakable mythical powers, in order to ascend again to the world of light, but he is in no single respect a man among men, nor does he share in their destiny (birth, suffering, and death).

3. The Redeemer whom Paul preaches sets aside his glory, humiliates himself, and takes on the figure of a servant, and becomes poor (Phil. 2; 2 Cor. 8). Nothing of what is said in these 'loci classici' supports Bultmann's theory of Christ, or is to be found in the Mandean myth. The hero who

descends from the world of light appears as one who is empowered against the powers. Bultmann knows very well how to modify all this. "The coming of the redeemer out of the world of light is a self-humiliation . . . and everything which souls now experience, was previously experienced by the redeemer in a primeval period . . . "[70] But this description is very precarious and cannot remove the fact that what Paul says in Philippians 2 over the voluntary self-humiliation of Christ is not in any way comparable with the hard-pressed heroes of the Mandeans, who are coerced by other forces. The word *Selbstentäuszerung* may therefore not be employed here!

4. The only thing which presents itself for comparison here is the very general idea of the descent of the pre-existent Son of God, as Paul in Philippians 2 and in other places describes the coming of Christ, and as in the gnostic myth, the coming of the pre-temporal, mythical figure of the heroes is presented. No one would dare to affirm, however, that Paul and John (or their predecessors) only arrived at the idea of the pre-existence of Christ and of his coming out of the heavens with the aid of this cosmological gnostic myth. And this is true even apart from the fact that it is completely unacceptable to think that they could have paganized their gospel in such a manner.

No other conclusion is possible than this: as long as one limits oneself to the Christological conceptions in Paul (or John), every notion which would seek a schema for these conceptions within this gnostic myth is fantastic and absurd. *The actual motif for this construction is then also of an entirely different nature.* What motivates Bultmann and others to arrive at such a conception of things is not the Christological conceptions of Paul but rather the anthropology which in his opinion lies at their foundation. Bultmann sees behind Pauline Christology and the gnostic 'redeemer's myth,' the same human *Seinsverständnis*, namely, the feeling of being threatened by cosmic 'powers,' the existential consciousness of being imprisoned and bound in a world in which one realizes himself to be alien in his deepest being or existence. On the basis of this *Existenzverständnis* Bultmann would understand the modality of the gnostic speculation and of Paul's doctrine of redemption. He sees between this two-fold vital feeling a difference but he also sees a far-reaching agreement. And in view of the fact that according to Bultmann the entire Christology of the New Testament, including that of Paul, is simply a mythological expression of the transcendental possibility of salvation from the previously described need, Bultmann believes that he can point to an analogy between Paul's Christology and the gnostic redemptive drama. The analogy is to be explained in terms of this common *Seinsverständnis*, by which the gnostic myth, provided the primary concepts for the Pauline (and Johannine) theory of redemption. The actual basis of the entire construction does not lie, therefore, in the same conception of the Redeemer, in Paul and in the gnosis, but it lies in the modern anthropological interpretation of both.

In our opinion in appraising this situation one must guard against being sidetracked and must retain the central question firmly in view. And the latter is not how far Paul, in his opposition to specific false syncretistic doctrines, sometimes approvingly employs their terminology in some of his letters, for example, in his epistle to the Colossians. The question is also not in the first place, how we must think of the 'powers' of which Paul speaks (perhaps also in agreement with non-Christian conceptions). The central question is rather whether we ought to understand Paul's Christology, especially his preaching of the descent of the pre-existent Son of God into the world, in any sense as an objectivization, for and in faith, of his anthropology, of his *Dase-*

insverständnis. And, on this point, the New Testament does not allow any room for doubt. Bultmann's explanation of Paul's Christology *in casu* of that which is stated in Philippians 2, and related places, of the descent of the pre-existent Son of God, can only be taken seriously, if one ascribes to Christ's heavenly form of existence no other significance than a mythological one. In contrast Bultmann's conception loses its rationality when this heavenly form of existence of Christ's is not accepted as a projection of Paul's believing *Daseinsverständnis* but is conceived of as a reality made known to him by divine revelation. It does not need to be demonstrated that Paul himself knew this heavenly existence of Christ from the unshakable certainty of the revelation which was given to him. The starting point of his Christology remains: "when it pleased God to reveal his Son to me." Herein also lies a sufficient explanation of what Paul writes concerning Christ's self-humiliation as the Son of God. For in this revelation there lay for him not only the certainty of Christ's *a posteriori* exaltation into the heavens, but no less the certainty of his previous descent from the heavens. For this conclusion Paul did not need any gnostic myths. For Christ was for Paul not only an intermediatory being exalted into the heavens by his death and resurrection. Christ the exalted one, was for Paul the Son of God, who in his exaltation returned to the place from which he came. Therefore, Christ's pre-existence is for Paul not a *Lehnsatz* (borrowed principle) from the then contemporary mythology. It is for him the implication of Christ's divine glory which he had learned to know by revelation. To say that the Pauline Christology is not to be understood apart from the presupposition of the gnostic Redeemer-mythos is, therefore, not only a thesis which cannot be demonstrated in terms of this gnostic myth, but in addition a thesis which is a misunderstanding of the actual source and origin of Paul's entire preaching of Christ: the revelation of God of his Son

Jesus Christ, and the knowledge of the historical Christ who humbled himself in death. That which Bultmann explains as mythical in this construction Paul clearly points to in his epistles with the greatest clarity as the fruit of revelation and as a knowledge of that which he had received from the tradition.[71]

The sole question which remains to be answered is whether or not Paul in speaking of Jesus' divine self-humiliation and descent from the heavens, essentially proclaimed anything new in comparison with Jesus' self-revelation, and the preaching of the early church; or otherwise stated: whether or not in Philippians 2 what Paul writes concerning Christ's humiliation and exaltation is to be understood within the development of what we have indicated up until now as the Christian *kerygma.*

To this must be answered that everything again depends here upon the value which one ascribes to the witness of the gospels concerning Jesus' preaching. From the gospels themselves it cannot be denied that Christ's pre-existence and therefore his coming from the heavens is either explicitly expressed (e.g., John 3:13, 17ff), or implicitly presupposed (e.g., the synoptic gospels). With respect to the synoptic gospels one can point to Jesus' self-witness concerning his coming and to his being sent (the so-called $\mathring{\eta}\lambda\theta o\nu$—and the $\mathring{a}\pi\epsilon\sigma\tau\acute{a}\lambda\eta\nu$ pronouncements). It is true that this expression taken by itself does not need to be viewed as an indication of Jesus' coming or his being sent 'from the heavens' and is thus no proof of his pre-existence (Cf. e.g., Matt. 11:18). From a closer examination of the content of these statements it appears, however, that they are more than expressions of a prophetic 'official consciousness of one's calling.'[72] What is here indicated is a coming out of the heavens to the earth (Cf. Luke 12:49), and the Son's being sent by the Father from the heavenly regions (Mark 12:6), and thus the reference is to the temporal 'existence' of Christ upon the earth (Mark 9:19).[73] In our opinion, all this, viewed in the light of the entire gospel, indicates an unmistakable reference to Christ's pre-existence. And even if one should think that this exegesis of the ἦλθον passages rests upon a weak basis,[74] there then remains, however, the fact that Jesus' messianic self-revelation bore such a powerful divine character, both before as well as in his resurrection, that in it is to be found the certain ground for the faith that not only is he the Son of God, exalted in the heavens, but that he also came from the heavens. The situation here is not to be judged by or in terms of a previously established *religionsgeschichtliche* schema. What is characteristic of Jesus' self-revelation is that in his coming fulfillment far exceeded in all respects expectation and did not permit itself to be explained in terms of any contemporary messianic or similar schema. What is decisive is not whether we can discover, in the preaching that we still have of the early Palestinian church, clear statements of pre-existence, but the issue is whether the foundation of such was laid in Jesus' messianic self-disclosure. And then it must be said that pre-existence is not to be separated from Jesus' glory as *Kyrios* and from his existence as the Son of God. And, that which Paul in Philippians 2 and 2 Corinthians 8 testifies concerning the self-humiliation and the voluntary poverty of the pre-existent Son of God is the expression of the faith and the preaching of the early church.

The same conclusions follows from what we observed at the outset of our study[75] concerning the two aspects of Jesus' revelation of his person and work, i.e., that of his messianic glory and of his self-humiliation. "The Son of Man has not come to be served, but in order to serve," is the synoptic counterpart of Philippians 2. The humiliation which Jesus consciously took upon himself is in the first place related to what happened on earth, in his self-conceal-ment, in his suffering and death and obedience to God's historical redemptive plan. Nevertheless, in the light of Jesus' consciousness of being 'the Son' and of possessing absolute divine power 'on the earth' (Matt. 9:6), all that happened to him on earth has a transcendent pre-existent background. Therefore, in the last analysis—from the standpoint of the reality of the fulfillment of redemption in Christ's coming—there is no reason to view the pre-existence and the descent of the Son of God from the heavens, as a Hellenistic *theologoumenon*, foreign to the original gospel. Rather, Christ's pre-existence, etc., is implied in Jesus' self-revelation and to the degree that the faith of the church became more conscious of its absolute significance, it necessarily formed the content of the Christian *kerygma*. Herein, and not in dependence upon all sorts of fantastic speculations of gnosticism—if such existed during the time of Paul—lies the 'natural' basic structure of Paul's theory of redemption: "There is really one way out of the difficulty. It is an old and radical way. But the world of scholarship may come back to it in the end. The fundamental difficulty in explaining the origin of Paul's religion will never disappear by being ignored; it will never yield to compromises of any kind. It will disappear only when Jesus is recognized as really being what Paul presupposed him to be and what all the gospels represent him as being—the eternal Son of God, come to earth for the redemption of man, now seated once more on the throne of his glory."[76]

19. *Jesus Christ and the Cosmos*

And now one more but closely related question, namely: To what extent does the cosmic significance ascribed by Paul to Christ, in the work of creation and redemption, introduce a new Christological doctrine, alien to the original gospel? In particular our concern is with the previously discussed passages[77] which speak of Christ's creative work

(1 Cor. 8:6, and especially Col. 1:15ff), as well as with the statements according to which something of a cosmic struggle is operative within the work of Christ, a struggle leading to a reconciliation of all things through Christ, the first born of the dead, and also of the entire creation (Col. 1:18ff, cf. 2:9).

Now a distinction must be made between the cosmic significance ascribed to Christ's redemptive work and to his exaltation in the heavens, and the significance ascribed to his creative work as the pre-existent Son of God. When in Philippians 2:10ff Paul says that to Christ as the exalted one, the entire cosmos, "both what is in the heavens and what is upon the earth, and what is under the earth" honor must be shown, and in Colossians 1:20 that through him the cosmos is reconciled, "that which is upon the earth and that which is in the heavens," then his words and concepts do not imply anything other than that which from the very beginning formed the content of the New Testament *kerygma*, not only according to the Gospel of John, but also according to the synoptic gospels and the book of Acts. Basically this all-inclusive power and glory, which Paul ascribes to Christ, is nothing other than that of the Son of Man (Daniel 7:14) with whom Jesus identifies himself in his self-disclosure.[78] Nowhere is this more explicitly stated than in the appearance of the resurrected Lord in Galilee (Matt. 20:18). This statement includes everything which forms the content of the title *Kyrios*[79] and it also discloses the cosmic significance of Christ's redemptive work, in the full sense. And that this statement refers to the spiritual world, to which Paul points in his epistles, is clear in itself, and evident to the fullest when viewed against the background of the gospel of Matthew, to which these words form the conclusion, as well as from the standpoint of the synoptic *kerygma* in general. The degree to which the work of Christ is described as a conflict with Satan appears

in the very start of Jesus' ministry when he was tempted
by the devil in the wilderness (Matt. 4:1ff). And this is
repeatedly visible, as frequently Jesus conducts the conflict
against the demons, especially when he speaks in the manner
of Matthew 12:25-30. The demons recognize him earlier
than man, and shudder at his coming, violently set themselves against him, and appeal to the fact that the 'time' is
still given to them to have power over creation (Cf. Mark
1:23ff; Luke 4:41ff; Matt. 8:29). It is true that in the
synoptic gospels the power of demons appears differently
than in that of John, especially with respect to the form of
possession. For in Paul and John the emphasis appears to
be more upon the cosmic and spiritual character of their
power and working (Cf., e.g., Eph. 6:12ff; John 12:31, etc.).
Nevertheless, even in the synoptic gospels the actual conflict
between Satan and man is of a religious and a moral nature
(Matt. 6:13), and does not work itself out merely in the
psychical and somatic life. And the motif of the cosmic
power of demons and Jesus' opposition to it does not only
appear at the end of the gospel but directly at the beginning
(Matt. 4:8ff; Luke 10:18).

To the question: How is this cosmic conflict to be viewed
within the framework of the New Testament *kerygma*?
Bultmann answers that, at least with respect to the *kerygma*
of the Hellenistic church (including Paul), the pre-Christian
gnosticism had a great influence here upon Christian thought,
and added to the development of the Christian theological
language. Bultmann seeks this influence in what he calls
the conceptual development of the eschatological dualism,
in the sense, that therein cosmological *thinking* is further
developed. The expectation of the future already acquired
cosmic dimensions in Jewish eschatology, under the influence
of the same Iranian, and Babylonian mythology, which also
formed the sources of mythological thinking of gnosticism.[80]

Within the framework of our study, concerned with the

Christological foundations of the New Testament *kerygma*,
it is not relevant to enter into the much discussed question
of the influence of the Eastern, especially of the Iranian
religion, on the Old Testament and non-canonical writings,
especially with respect to cosmology and demonology. It
seems irrefutable, however, that Paul does not base his
Christology upon the motifs of a more or less dualistic
cosmology, but rather upon the *history of salvation*, which
finds its foundation in the creation of the world. The notion
that the conflict between Jesus and Satan bears the character
of a cosmic myth, in which man is not guilty so much because
of sin, but rather is a sacrifice to fate, is not to be found in
Paul any more than in the synoptic gospels. In the synoptic
gospels the temptation of Jesus by Satan apparently functions as a counterpart to the temptation of the first man in
paradise; something of the paradise situation even recurs
by way of contrast in the wilderness (Cf. Mark 1:13). The
main issue of the conflict is, therefore, not a victory over a
'cosmic dualism,' the redemption of man from powers which
control him, but it is the re-establishment of that which has
been disturbed by sin. Likewise, the *character* of the struggle is not a test of power between mythical figures, but
rather it is a moral temptation to disobedience. The power
of Jesus over Satan and the world, according to the synoptic
gospels and according to John, rests upon the obedience of
Christ to the will of the Father (Cf. Matt. 4:8ff and 28:18).
All this is not controlled by dualistic mythological themes,
but by redemptive-historical motives.

The same thing is true of Paul. No matter to what
extent Paul may have been influenced by the thought or
terminology of Hellenism, and may have placed himself in
the thought world of his readers, it is certain that he did
not replace or denature the redemptive historical element by
the cosmological element. Rather it appears again and again
in Paul how much the cosmic dimension of Christ's redemp-

tive work is the direct consequence of his redemptive historical preaching. When as in Romans 8:19, Paul portrays with
penetrating words the need of the entire created life within
the cosmos, he is undoubtedly convinced that what is here
operative is the death and curse which entered the world
through sin (Rom. 5:12ff). And when he reflects upon the
significance of Christ's redemption, he returns again and
again to the beginning of history, especially in developing
the parallel between Adam and Christ (Rom. 5:12-21; 1 Cor.
15:45-49). Herein is not operative, as some will again have
us believe, a motif out of pagan cosmologies, according to
which the primeval man has fallen into the power of the
rulers of the world opposed to God, and as a result man, in
his deepest being, knows himself to be constantly alien to
the mode of being of this world. Rather Paul bases his point
of view upon the fulfillment of the history of redemption in the
coming of Christ, and for this reason he not only draws a
parallel between Christ and Moses and Christ and Abraham,
but also between Christ and Adam. Moreover, Paul is not
concerned with the cosmos with all its unsolved needs, because man was once sacrificed to hostile powers in control
of the world. The opposite is the case, because of the
sin of man the cosmos is also subjected to the 'vanity' and
'the bondage of corruption,' and therefore longingly looks for-
ward to be readopted as the children of God (Rom. 8:19ff).
Undoubtedly by sin man has also become powerless. His
situation cannot simply be described in terms of sin and
guilt; an adequate description needs also to speak of calamity,
disaster, bondage, subjection. But this powerlessness is the
consequence of his guilt, and the latter works itself out in the
former. Therefore, for Paul the redemption which appeared
in Christ is of a cosmic nature. The idea of redemption is
accompanied by the notion of creation which lies at its
foundation and forms the background of Paul's great redemptive-historical vision. The 'vital feeling' of the period,[81] in

which the apostle lived, could have confronted him strongly
with the problem: man and the cosmos, and in Paul's
eschatology, the cosmic stands more in the foreground than
in that of the prophets. But all this does not remove the
fact that the basic structure of these cosmic-soteriological
and cosmic-Christological statements are completely an-
chored in Biblical thought. The boundary lines of redemption coincide with those of the cosmos, for the cosmos is
from the beginning, the creation and property of the Lord
(1 Cor. 10:26).

The statements concerning Christ's original relation
to the creation ought to be understood in close connection
with what we have just said. It is evident from the prologue
of John as well as from Hebrews 1:3 and Revelation 3:14,
that we are not here confronted with a peculiarity of Paul's
Christology. It cannot be stated, however, whether and to
what degree this idea was already present within the early
Palestinian church. In what we read in the book of Acts,
this idea does not come to the fore, nor is there anything in
Jesus' self-revelation in the gospels that points in this direction. Judging on the basis of what is known in the gospels
of Jesus preaching, we must say that the notion of the
'mediator' of creation actually constitutes a new element in
the Christology of Paul.

In every conceivable way an attempt has been made to
find a point of contact for this idea, in pre-Christian literature,
within the Old Testament, and in non-canonical and pagan
writings. We can in the main distinguish four attempts to
find a common root or origin.[82]

1. It has been thought that a kinship could be found—
even if not a direct and demonstrable one—between Paul's
preaching of Christ, as the Image of God and the First Born
of all creatures, and the cosmological speculations of Philo.
It is pointed out that in Philo the world of ideas is also
described as the Son of God and that, on the other hand,

the equivalent logos is called the πρωτόγονος and τῶν ἀγγέλων πρεσβύτατος and is identified with the primeval man created in the image of God. Of this Logos or Son of God it is said that he is the ἀρχὴ καὶ ὄνομα θεοῦ καὶ λόγος, καὶ ὁ κατ᾽ εἰκόνα ἄνθρωπος. In this conception the κόσμος νοητός, the Logos, the ideal man, is thus an intermediary stage between God and the visible world. It is generally recognized, however, that the conceptual world of Philo (who was strongly under the influence of Plato) and that of Paul, are very far from each other. The idea of a mediator who bridges the distance between God and the cosmos is completely and entirely alien to Paul, as is also the idealistic conception of a κόσμος νοητός and a Logos as an hypostatized objectivization of the divine ideas. In Paul, Christ's mediatorship of creation is not, as in Philo, the fruit of a cosmological speculation. The starting point of Paul's pronouncements lie rather in the being-equal-with-God of the incarnate and exalted Christ; it lies in the historical revelation of Christ as God's Son.

2. It is thought that another parallel can be found in the cosmological conception of the so-called Hermetic literature.[83] One here encounters the cosmos (κόσμος), as an intermediary stadium between God and man. This cosmos is then also called the Son and Image of God. And on the other hand, man is then the Son of the cosmos.[84] No one can affirm—viewed in itself—that there is in all this to be found any striking similarity or agreement with the statements of Paul. Also here the basic idea is that of a bridging over of the transcendent God and the empirical world, an idea which is entirely lacking in Paul. One must view the entire agreement as concentrated in the word εἰκών which, in our opinion, is a point of comparison which is far too external.

3. Also in this connection[85] the attempt is made by various expositors to explain Paul's Christology in terms of gnosticism. In the cosmological-soteriological conception

of primeval man, which is of Iranian origin, and which can
be reconstrued from Mandesean and Manichean texts,
Dibelius, for example, has tried to find the same connection
between cosmology and soteriology, which is so characteristic
of Paul. It is, however, not clear how one can relate this
to the creative work of Christ. For the idea that the world
in its totality is *created* by God or a heavenly being, and is
subordinate to him in rank, is alien to the pessimistic dualism
of gnosticism. Even the souls or components of light are not
the creation of the primeval man or of the descended
redeemer; they are the divine sparks of light fallen into
matter. In short, all such conceptions, with respect to their
concrete form and basic ideas, are entirely alien to what
Paul says (Col. 1 and 1 Cor. 8), and one can only be
surprised at the certainty and ease with which such otherwise critical scholars as Dibelius and Bultmann here see
parallels and find connections.[86]

4. By far the most important parallel form to be mentioned in this connection is that of the Wisdom of Proverbs
8:22. Many who reject as an analogy what is introduced from
Philo or the gnostic literature, are of the opinion that in
Colossians 1:15ff, it is highly probable that Paul here unites
with the notions of Wisdom.[87] It is undeniable that even
if there is no equality here, there is, nevertheless, an agreement of terminology and ideas, and that of everything advanced as a point of comparison, the pronouncements concerning Wisdom display by far the most kinship with those
concerning Christ's creative activity. A short survey of the
material which is here relevant gives a clear impression of
this.[88]

In Proverbs 8, Wisdom says: "The Lord possessed me
in the beginning of his way, before his works of old.[89] I was
set up from everlasting from the beginning, or ever the
earth was formed. When there were no depths, I was
brought forth . . . before the mountains . . . before the hills

was I brought forth . . . when he prepared the heavens,
I was there and when he appointed the foundations of the
earth: then was I by him, as one brought up with him
(according to other lections and translation: 'as a master
workman').[90] Rejoicing in the habitable part of his earth
(vs. 23-31)." Here pre-existence is ascribed to Chochma
(Wisdom.) Also one may assume or accept the fact that
according to this conception the Chochma (Wisdom) was
present at the creation of the world, and through it God
brought about creation.[91] In the apocrypha and pseudepi-
graphic literature, these ideas of Wisdom are again brought
to the fore and worked out more fully. Thus, for example, in
the Wisdom of Jesus Sirach, 1:4: "before all things is Wisdom
created."[92] (Cf. also vs. 9, 14; as also in 24:3, where Wisdom
is portrayed as the cloud which moves or swerves over and
fructifies the earth.) Especially, however, in the book of
Wisdom of Solomon (Sapientia), is Wisdom described as the
architect of all things[93] (7:21), as a breath[94] of God's power,
as a result[95] of his glory, as a ray of the eternal light,[96] and
the image[97] of his goodness (7:25ff), as the co-regent of
God[98] (9:4); it was present when God created the world
(9:9). It can be said in summary that Wisdom was created
by God before the creation, is an image of God, and shares
in the creation of the world. For some the kinship between
that which is said of the Wisdom and Colossians 1:15ff,
2 Corinthians 4:4; 1 Corinthians 8:6, is so evident that one
can assume with certainty that Paul clothed the messianic
Jesus with the halo of Jewish Wisdom.[99] Also the fact that
these conceptions originate in the Old Testament writings
makes it much easier to see here a certain dependence of
Paul's ideas than in the case of pagan speculations.[100]

Nevertheless, an attitude of reserve ought to be adopted.
Whoever seriously considers the nature of the pronouncements concerning Wisdom, and is not led away by the sound
of several words, such as the 'image of God's' (goodness),

etc., sees that Paul in Colossians 1, and in similar places, did not simply reproduce existing conceptions and transfer them to Jesus.

Of no little significance is the fact that nowhere in the Old Testament, nor in later Judaism is this Wisdom figure in Proverbs 8 equated with the Messiah, nor have the characteristics with which Proverbs describes Wisdom been transferred to the Messiah.[101] Thus, in Colossians 1:15ff, Paul does not operate with traditional messianic attributes. On the other hand there is no proof that he himself views Jesus Christ as the pre-existent Wisdom of Proverbs 8. Not only does Paul never cite such passages as Proverbs 8 (and such books as Sirach and Sapientia) but also the figure of Wisdom which appears therein does not occur in his epistles. Paul does say that Christ (in addition to other gifts, also) has become Wisdom for us (1 Cor. 1:30, cf. vs. 24, 2:6; Col. 2:3). Yet it is clear that this is something entirely different than the identification of Christ with the pre-existent figure of Wisdom; and, on the other hand, just where it is thought that this identification can be encountered (as in Col. 1; 1 Cor. 8; 2 Cor. 4), no mention is made of Wisdom. This ought to make us very careful not to posit a connection between Proverbs 8 and Colossians 1, too eagerly and easily.

It is, moreover, also evident that the figure of Wisdom in Proverbs 8 clearly bears the character of a 'half abstract'[102] personification, and not that of a person. There is in the *chochmatic* literature no question of the existence of Wisdom as God, as it occurs in Paul's epistles with respect to Christ, and as it is spoken of in John of the Logos. Everything said in the Wisdom literature of this Wisdom is simply a poetic description of the virtue of the divine Wisdom, with which God created the world, and of which the wise exalt the gifts for human life. The same occurs *mutatis mutandis* in the rabbinical literature of Torah.[103] In this light there is then also an essential difference, when it is said in the Wisdom literature that the Wisdom was the architect with God, before the creation of the world (Prov. 8:30) (LXX), and in the Sap. 7:21), that it is the architect of all things, and when Paul says of Christ, that by him all things were created. What in the first instance is a personification of God's virtue, is in Paul the pre-existent person of the Son of God, who came to earth in the man Jesus Christ. Christ is not simply the instrument or the power which God employs in the creation of the world, but the entire cosmos finds in him its continual existence, and all things are not only in him, and through him, but all things are created for him, i.e., they find in him also their end and goal. In all this the person and significance of Christ, with respect to the cosmos, far exceeds what is said in the *chochmatic* literature of Wisdom.[104] In Paul—and this is the actual difference—the pre-existent creative work of the Son of God is never abstracted, even for a moment, from the person of Jesus Christ, who came in the flesh, and who through his suffering and death, is exalted in the heavens, and who had revealed himself to Paul, as the glorified Lord. The 'Mediator' of creation is for Paul not a personification, not an hypostasis, but the revealed Son of God.

It is for this reason that what Paul in Colossians 1 and elsewhere says of the creative work of Christ, as the Son of God, is difficult to conceive of as a messianic interpretation of certain *chochmatic* texts. What he says follows for Paul out of the single but overwhelming fact that Christ in his very essence is the Son of God. There is, therefore, between the Father and the Son, a fellowship or sharing of life and operations, so that the expression 'in him and through him and to him' is applicable not only of the Father but also of the Son.[105] The Son is always the Image of (invisible) God (2 Cor. 4:4; Col. 1:15), whereby again we must not in the first place seek a universal *religionsgeschichtliche* or Old Testament parallel, or other points of contact,[106]

but in the first place must think of the tremendous revelatory
reality of the divine glory in Jesus Christ. For Paul the
creation and the sustaining of the cosmos by God was the
foundation of the entire history of redemption. For this
reason the relation of Christ to the cosmos was given with
his divine pre-existence. Noetically, the soteriological aspect
may take preference, in the sense that the Son of God
reveals himself as the Redeemer of the world. On the other
hand, however, Christ because he is the Son, is also the Lord
of the cosmos in both creation and redemption. What Paul
says of Christ's creative work is not a strange cosmological
addition to his doctrine of redemption, whether of a speculative Greek or a gnostic-existentialist nature. Nor is it a
soteriological postulate, in the sense that according to Paul
(and John) the world is created by the Son of God, because
he also is the Redeemer of the world.[107] Rather, in these
pronouncements the unity of the divine work of creation
and redemption is expressed and therefore nothing in heaven
and upon earth withdraws itself from the redeeming rule of
Christ, because the Redeemer came to *his own* world. The
expressions, 'through him' and 'in him' and 'to him' mutually
modify each other. Witness to this unity is not only borne
with respect to the divine work but also to the *person* of
Christ, as the basis and realization of this unity. And such
is not to be explained in terms of any pre-Christian messianic or *religionsgeschichtlich* schema, but in terms of the
fulness of God's revelation in Christ, of which Paul together
with the other apostles is the witness and the preacher.

The latter is true with respect to the general tenor and
basic idea of these pronouncements. One can thereby observe that the manner in which this is brought to expression
is more *special* and unique than that of the participation of
the Son in the creative omnipotence and Wisdom of God.

In summary, especially with respect to the cosmic significance ascribed by Paul to the pre-existent Christ, a notable

progress is ascertainable when a comparison is made with what the gospels, in particular the synoptics, disclose of Jesus' self-revelation. Nevertheless, from the preceding it is clearly evident that that which is expressed of Christ's work as the Creator of the world, is not a *corpus-alienum* or a speculative addition to the original gospel. On the contrary it forms the supreme explication and consequence of the original gospel. On the one hand, it is the absolute significance of Christ's person, which expresses itself here in the conscious faith of the New Testament revelatory witnesses and of the church. And this absoluteness of Christ's person is the origin and foundation of his self-revelation. He is the Emmanuel (Matt. 1:23). Therefore, no attribute of God can and may be denied to him. But therefore, the content of this self-revelation of God in Christ is not at once unfolded in all its implications. On the other hand, the unification of the Christological and the cosmic has as its foundation the final and deepest presupposition of the New Testament gospel preaching: the faith that the entire cosmos is created by God and is under the dominion of his sovereign laws. This fundamental datum of the revelation of God according to the Scriptures, the foundation also of Jesus' preaching of the kingdom of heaven, is again visible in the revelation of the Son of God, now, however, in the full light of the divine redemptive work. In this sense one can say that the divine work of creation is correctly revealed only in redemption. But on the other hand, the length and the breadth, the depths and heights of Christ's redemptive work is only visible in the entire cosmos, in that which is visible and invisible, and that which is in the heaven and that which is on the earth. In redemption God returns to his creation. This is the mainspring of the gospel as the gospel of the kingdom. It is also the conclusion of the latter, when Paul in opposition to all demonic usurpation of power, and pagan anxiety, preaches

Jesus Christ, as the Son of God, in whom, through whom, and to whom everything is created, the First Born *of all creatures,* as he also is the beginning, the first born *from the dead* (Col. 1:15, 18).

NOTES

NOTES

CHAPTER I

[1] For the history of the problem see: A. Schweitzer, *Geschichte der Paulinischen Forschung* (1933), pp. 119ff; P. Feine, *Der Apostel Paulus* (1927), 158ff; R. Bultmann, *Zur Geschichte der Paulus-Forschung, Theol. Rundschau*, N. F. (1929), pp. 26-59; idem. *Neuste Paulus-Forschung, Theol. Rundschau*, N. F. (1936), pp. 1-22.

[2] For the liberal view the following titles are representative: H. J. Holtzmann, *Lehrbuch der neutest. Theologie II* (1911), see, for example, pp. 235ff, 257ff; J. Weiss, *Jesus im glauben des Urchristentums* (1910); Ad. Jülicher, *Paulus und Jesus* (1907).

[3] Cf. H. Ridderbos, *Zelfopenbaring en Zelfverberging* (1946), pp. 7ff.

[4] *Paulus* (1907), p. 48.

[5] *Ibid.*, p. 53.

[6] *Ibid.*, p. 103.

[7] *Ibid.*, p. 104.

[8] *Ibid.*, pp. 90ff.

[9] *Ibid.*, pp. 72, 84.

[10] *Ibid.*, p. 104.

[11] *Ibid.*, pp. 84ff.

[12] On the basis of 2 Cor. 5:16 it is frequently asserted that Jesus made a deep impression on Paul during his earthly life. Thus J. Weiss, *op. cit.*, pp. 23ff, writes: "A personality (like Jesus'), who inspired such enthusiasm and such hatred, simply must have drawn the attention of such an earnest and important man as Paul; and this in a purely human way, by his outward appearance and manner; his countenance and the look in his eye, his word and his gestures. . . . Paul's experience is inconceivable without such direct or indirect contact with Jesus. . . . He must have had and actually did have, a bright and lively image of the ethical and religious personality of Jesus."

[13] Thus, for example, Holtzmann, following the lead of other scholars, would explain Paul's conception of Christ as an objectivization and generalization of his subjective experience at Damascus. He writes, *op. cit.* II, p. 238: "the whole of St. Paul's 'doctrine' (about the significance of Christ) will only be intelligible and transparent from the point of view that it is the generalization of what its author had gone through in his own person and what he, therefore, enjoins on all who follow the same path as something

they should share. It simply means the explanation of the content of Paul's conversion, the systematization of the Christophany."

14 Wrede, *op cit.*, p. 87.

15 *Ibid.*, p. 89.

16 *Ibid.*, p. 96.

17 H. Gunkel, *Zum religionsgeschichtlichen Verständnis des Neuen Testaments* (1930), p. 89.

18 *Ibid.*, p. 90.

19 *Ibid.*, p. 92.

20 *Ibid.*, pp. 93ff.

21 *Ibid.*, p. 95.

22 *Ibid.*, p. 89.

23 Of special importance in this connection is the work of M. Bruckner, *Die Entstehung der paulinischen Christologie* (1903). See also—in the line of Gunkel—Max Maurenbrecher, *Von Jerusalem nach Rom*, cf. A. Schweitzer *op. cit.*, p. 181.

24 Cited by *Firmicus Maternus*, Christian author of the 4th century, who wrote a work against the Eastern mystery religions, *De errore profanarum religionum;* see XXII.

25 See his Essay on "Todestaufe und Christliche Ethik" in *An die Römer* (1933), pp. 65ff, and especially p. 67.

26 Ad Autolukon I, 9: καὶ ταῦτα μὲν μέτριον εἰπεῖν, ὅπου γε θεὸς εὑρίσκεται μεμελισμένος ὁ καλούμενος ᾽Οσιρις, οὗ καὶ κατ᾽ ἔτός γίνονται τελεταὶ ὡς ἀπολλυμένου καὶ εὑρισκομένου καὶ κατὰ μέλος ζητουμένου οὔτε γὰρ εἰ ἀπόλλυται νοεῖται, οὔτε εἰ εὑρίσκεται δείκνυται.

27 In his book *Kyrios Christos* (1913) (1921). For the significance of Bousset see also A. Schweitzer, *Die Mystik des Apostels Paulus* (1930), pp. 30-37; R. Bultmann, *Glauben und Verstehen* (1933), pp. 252-256, and especially J. Gresham Machen, *The Origin of Paul's Religion* (1947) (1921), pp. 257ff.

28 *Op. cit.*, p. 125.

29 "In its environment early Christianity could not help but assume this form of *Kyrios* worship and *Kyrios* belief, there was no other possibility," Bousset, *op. cit.*, p. 124.

30 See chapter 5.

31 For his criticism of Bousset see *Glauben und Verstehen* (1933), p. 256; also his *Zur Geschichte des Paulus-Forschung, Theol. Rundschau*, N. F. (1929), pp. 50ff.

32 *Die Mystik des Apostels Paulus* (1930), pp. 89ff.

33 *Op. cit.*, p. 337.

34 Cf. his *Jesus und Paulus* in *Jesus Christus im Zeugnis der Heiligen Schrift und der Kirche* (1936), p. 84; see also his article *Neueste Paulus-Forschung, op. cit.*, p. 10, and his *Die Bedeutung des geschichtlichen Jesus für die Theologie des Paulus* in *Glauben und Verstehen* (1933), pp. 191ff.

35 *Theologie des Neuen Testaments* I (1948), p. 8.

[36] *Op. cit.* p. 44: "Jesus' call for a decision implies a Christology."

[37] *Theologie*, pp. 166ff; see also his *Das Urchristentum im Rahmen der antiken Religionen* (1949), pp. 182ff.

[38] Cf. Bultmann, *Neueste Paulus-Forschung, Theol. Rundschau* N. F. (1936), pp. 18ff. Bultmann agrees with Bousset that this gnostic piety is especially prevalent in the mystery religions, *Das Urchristentum* (1949), pp. 196ff. However, Bultmann is not willing to explain Christology as a projection of the mystery cults, nor in terms of the myths of the cults (e.g., the myth of the dying and re-living of Osiris). Rather he seeks its explanation in the gnostic "Seinsverständnis (understanding of existence), according to the analogy of the myth of the redeemed Redeemer.

[39] *Gnosis und spätantiker Geist*, I (1934).

[40] In the second part of his *Theol. des N. T.* (1951), Bultmann bases the existence of a pre-Christian gnosticizing Judaism on the manuscripts recently found in Palestine, p. 361. For the theological content of these writings see: W. Baumgartner, *Der palästinische Handschriftenfund, Theol. Runschau* (1951), pp. 97ff.

[41] Cf. his *Neues Testament und Mythologie* in *Kerygma und Mythos* (1948), especially pp. 33ff.

CHAPTER II

[1] Cf. *Kerygma und Mythos* (1948), pp. 24ff, where Bultmann discusses and rejects earlier efforts to demythologize (namely those of liberal theology and of the *religionsgeschichtliche* school).

[2] Thus in Bultmann's older writing *Jesus* (1929), pp. 12, 13: "Personally I am of the opinion that Jesus did not take himself to be the Messiah, but I do not imagine that such a view enables me to form a clearer picture of his personality. In what follows I have not considered this question, not because after all there is nothing to say about it with certainty, but because I think the question is immaterial." Likewise in *Glauben und Verstehen* (1933), pp. 256, 266: "Whether he knew he was the Messiah or not is of no consequence. It could only mean that he conceived of his work as being of the nature of a decision in the terms of a contemporary Jewish conception."

[3] Cf. also Herbert Braun in his treatment of Bultmann's *Theologie des N. T.* in *Verkündigung und Forschung* (1951), pp. 49-67, especially pp. 52, 63.

[4] *Theol. des N. T.*, p. 26.

[5] See for the following Bultmann's *Neues Testament und Mythologie*, in *Kerygma und Mythos*, edit. by H. W. Bartsch (1948). See also my *Enige grondmotieven van de theologie van Rudolf Bultmann*, in *Vox Theologica* (1950), pp. 33-46.

[6] "It is, therefore, impossible to believe in Christ first and then in his cross; belief in Christ means belief in the cross as the cross of Christ. Not because of the fact that it is the cross of Christ does it constitute the

occurrence of our salvation, but because being the occurrence of our salvation it is the cross of Christ. Apart from this it is the tragic end of a noble human personality." *Kerygma und Mythos,* p. 50. It is nowhere more evident than in this passage that for Bultmann Jesus' messiahship, his sonship, etc., are not the ground of belief but are rather the product of faith. No less characteristic of this absolute subjectivization of New Testament Christology is that which Bultmann writes concerning the deity of Christ. Bultmann raises the question as to how far this predicate is applied in the New Testament to the nature of Jesus, rather than to his *significance* for humanity. "Does he help me because he is the Son of God? Or is he the Son of God because he helps me?" And he answers: "Well, I believe it may be said that in the New Testament, at least *a parte potiori,* the statements about Jesus' divinity or deity are really statements concerning his significance, not concerning his nature." The extent to which Bultmann goes is evident when it is seen that this subjectivism is at the same time to be understood in an existentialistic and actualistic sense: "In the same way that the *ecclesia,* the church, the eschatological congregation, is only a real *ecclesia* as an occurrence (*Ereignis*), so also is Christ's being the Lord, his deity, also only an occurrence." Thus Christ's deity consists solely in the fact that he is repeatedly made to be divine by our faith in him. Cf. Bultmann's *Das Christologische Bekenntnis des Oekumenischen Rates,* in *Evangelische Theologie,* II Jhrg. (1951/52), pp. 1-13, especially pp. 5, 6, 10.

⁷ See H. Ridderbos, *De Komst van het Koninkrijk,* pp. 35ff. An English translation of this work is being undertaken by the Presbyterian and Reformed Publishing Co.

⁸ Cf. Also W. Wiesner, *Anthropologisch oder theologische Schriftauslegung* in *Evangelische Theologie* (1950), p. 59: "The New Testament points the other way: only because it is the cross of Christ, the Son of God, it is the occurrence of our salvation, else it would be the death of a noble human being who could not help us."

⁹ A radical criticism of the Bible tries to avoid this by distinguishing the genuinely historical, the historically authentic, from the religiously authentic and the theologically important, in the Jesus tradition. Thus in the article *"Bibelautorität und Bibelkritk"* (Zeits. f. Theol. u. Kirche), p. 84. Erich Dinkler writes: "It is uncertain and subject to serious doubt whether or not Jesus knew and preached that He was the Messiah. But the unshakable foundation of our faith is the fact that Jesus was the Messiah and the Word of God to us. To couple the denial of the Messiah's self-consciousness with the denial of his divine sonship, or to draw conclusions from the former to the latter would mean no less than to deprive Christianity of the whole of its foundation." The latter is actually the case. Only it is not evident how Dinkler can escape this consequence in view of the fact that, at least according to the New Testament, the foundation of Christendom cannot be religiously genuine, unless it is also historically genuine (I John 1:1ff). When from the fact that the authority of the Bible is for our faith not dependent upon historical criticism, Dinkler concludes "that the truth of the faith is independent of the correctness of historical, critical

elucidation," he follows a logic which is in conflict with that of the New Testament.

[10] For this see the articles of G. C. Berkouwer, *Het Stilzwijgen* in Geref. Weekblad (1950), 5, 6, and 7.

[11] For a more extended discussion, see H. Ridderbos, *op. cit.*, pp. 88-101, and the literature cited there.

[12] *Theologie des New Testament*, p. 26.

[13] *Ibid.*, pp. 27ff.

[14] This also is applicable to the gospel of John, cf. 5:28ff; 6:54; notwithstanding the denial of W. Bauer in *Handbuch Zum N.T.* II (1912), p. 38; and especially of Bultmann in his *Die Eschatologie des Johannes Evangeliums* in *Glauben und Verstehen* (1933), pp. 134, 152, and in his *Evangelium des Johannes* (1950), pp. 111-2, where he says that in the gospel of John "the naive old Jewish-Christian and gnostic eschatology is abundant." Such passages as John 5:25ff and 12:48 which deny this are then viewed as a product of a later editor. Thus, also Bauer.

[15] *Ibid.*, pp. 29-30.

[16] Also by such authors as C. H. Dodd and J. Jeremias is this pointed out. See Ridderbos, *op. cit.*, pp. 386ff.

[17] For this two-fold unity in the gospel of John, see also Bultmann, *Theologie des N.T.*, II (1951), pp. 397ff. Bultmann calls this the *Paradoxie des Offenbarungsgedankens*, and he incorrectly believes that John was the first to be aware of it.

[18] *Ibid.*, p. 31.

[19] R. Otto, *Reich Gottes und Menschensohn*, pp. 209ff.

[20] G. Dalman, *Jesus Jeschua* (1929), p. 110.

[21] W. Manson, *Jesus the Messiah* (1943), pp. 31ff.

[22] W. Wrede, *Das Messiasgeheimnis* (1901) (1913).

[23] Even though this element is not lacking in John. Cf. Bultmann, *Theologie des N.T.* II (1951), p. 393.

[24] Bultmann, *Glauben und Verstehen*, p. 262.

[25] See, for example, Strack-Billerbeck, *Kommentar Zum N.T. aus Talmud und Midrasch* II (1924), pp. 273ff; W. Bousset, *Die Religion des Judentums im Späthellenistischen Zeitalter* (1926), p. 231.

[26] Cf. also J. Gresham Machen: "At first sight, the parallel between these Gods and Jesus may seem striking. Jesus also was represented as dying and as coming back to life again. But what is the significance of the parallel? Can it mean that the entire New Testament story of the death and resurrection of Jesus was derived from these vegetation myths? Such has been the conclusion of certain modern scholars. But of course this conclusion is absurd, and it is not favored by Bousset. The essential historicity of the crucifixion of Jesus under Pontius Pilate and of the rise of the belief in His resurrection among his intimate friends, stands too firm to be shaken by any theory of dependence upon pagan myth. Thus the argument drawn from the parallel between the New Testament story

and the pagan myth of the dying and rising god proves too much." *The Origin of Paul's Religion* (1947) (1925), p. 313.

27 For this view which is especially developed by John Weiss, see the extensive elaboration of Sevenster, *Christologie*, pp. 309ff.

28 Cf. Bauernfeind, *op. cit.*, p. 51: "The sole fact that Jesus was made the Lord need not at all mean that before his exaltation, as Lord, Jesus had merely been a human being like others; according to the analogy of Phil. 2:5ff we could better add that his state as a servant was only determined by his voluntary humiliation, but that from the very first he had the 'Divine Form,' as his own."

29 Cf. Bauernfeind. Lucas did not intend this, but behind this formula, taken over by Luke from the language of the church, stands "a longer quasi-adoptionistic history."

30 Compare also Sevenster, *op. cit.*, p. 311. He speaks of a complete revelation or disclosure of that which was already an actuality as a mystery, Grosheide, *De Handelingen der Apostelen* I, 1942, points out that ποιεῖν can also mean constituted as, revealed as, p. 85.

31 See also here Bauernfeind, *op. cit.*, p. 176. He admits that Luke would have hardly hit upon the idea of placing the beginning (this day) of the divine Sonship proper only at the resurrection instead of dating it earlier. This is why we must refer to a pre-Lukan theology. But if for Luke such an expression does not conflict with his own conception of Jesus' messiahship it is not evident why we must here accept a deviating pre-Lukan theologoumenon.

32 *Op. cit.*, p. 310.

33 Grosheide wishes to understand ἀναστήσας in vs. 33 in the general sense of the begetting of Jesus, and he points in support of this to 3 vs. 26. He admits, however, that this word is used intentionally because the promise concerning the Messiah is fulfilled in the resurrection, *op. cit.*, p. 431.

34 Bauernfeind also recognizes this *op. cit.*, pp. 46, 220.

35 See also in addition N. B. Stonehouse: *The Witness of Luke to Christ* (1951), pp. 165ff.

36 In this spirit, for example, Bauernfeind, *op. cit.*, p. 51. "Anyone who adopted Christological words from reliable sources had probably not always considered their possible consequences." This would also have been the case with Luke's writing down of the words: καὶ κύριον αὐτὸν καὶ χριστὸν ἐποίησεν ὁ θεός.

CHAPTER III

1 See the previous citation from John Weiss. See further for this view the survey of O. Kietzig in *Die Bekehrung des Paulus* (1932), pp. 110ff.

2 See for the different conceptions, for example, E. B. Allo, *Saint Paul Seconde Epitre aux Corinthiens* (1937), pp. 179ff; H. Lietzmann-W. G. Kümmel, *An die Korinther* I, II (1949), p. 205.

3 For a slightly different view, F. W. Grosheide, *De Tweede brief van den*

Apostel Paulus aan de Kerk te Korinthe (1939), pp. 205ff who rejects, however, the explanation that Paul is here speaking of his former acquaintance with Jesus.

⁴ This is still stronger if one may correctly presume that Paul here reacts against a reproach of his opponents that he had never seen Jesus. And this conception is more probable than that we here have to deal with an entirely unintentional (and nowhere repeated!) allusion to Paul's acquaintance with Jesus in the time prior to his conversion. Cf. Marcus Barth, *Der Augenzeuge* (1946), pp. 6, 101ff, 314ff.

⁵ See below section 12.

⁶ Thus W. Bousset, with respect to 2 Cor. 5:16, in his *Die Schriften des N.T.* II (1917), p. 195, observes "In these few statements we are confronted with the whole of the difficult problem about the relation of St. Paul's religion to the Gospel of Jesus."

⁷ ἔκτρωμα, premature birth, miscarriage; cf. for the various conceptions, Schneider, T W B II, p. 463ff. Most commonly it is viewed as a qualification of the manner in which Paul became a Christian. One then finds the agreement in the abnormal and in the tremendous. The objection against this is that ἔκτρωμα does not indicate or refer to one who is born too late but one who is born too early, the fruit of an abortion. Therefore, others wish to conceive of the term as (applied to him by his opponents?) a word of abuse by which Paul's spiritual unworthiness is indicated. Others view it only as a humiliating self reference of the apostle, without casting any reflection upon his spiritual birth, cf. Lietzmann-Kummel, *op. cit.*, p. 192.

⁸ ὤφθη. This word lays emphasis more upon the revelatory character of the event at Damascus than upon the visual. Cf. Michaelis, TWB V, p. 359, ὁράω.

⁹ In distinction from other personal visionary ecstatic experiences, cf. 2 Cor. 12:1ff.

¹⁰ ἐν ἐμσι probably ought to be translated simply by 'to me,' cf. 1 Tim. 1:16, or as the replacing of the single dative: 'me,' cf. Rom. 1:19; 1 Cor. 14:11; 2 Cor. 4:3. In verbs of knowing and making known ἐν does not refer only to the person through whom the communication is made or given, but also to the one who receives it. Cf. Blasz-Debrunner, *Grammatik des neutestam. Griechisch* (1943), pp. 220, 1; Preuschen-Bauer, *Wörterbuch zum N.T.* (1928), Sp. 406, IV, 4a; Oepke, TWB p. 535, see further ἐν; see also *Der Brief des Paulus an die Galater* (1937), p. 25.

¹¹ Incorrectly Markus Barth, *op. cit.* p. 158 considers that Gal. 1:12ff, does not have a relationship only to the event at Damascus. The context vs. 16, 17ff, proves this expressly.

¹² Cf. Michaelis, *op. cit.*, pp. 360-1. In our opinion it is not certain that Paul, in the hour of his conversion at Damascus became directly conscious of his calling as an apostle to the heathen, as is affirmed by K. Pieper, *Paulus* (1929), pp. 42ff.

¹³ For the different conceptions of Paul's conversion from the perspective of his personal religious development, see especially O. Kietzig, *Die Bekehrung des Paulus* (1932), pp. 51-72, and further E. Phaff, *Die Bekehrung des Paulus in der Exegese des 20 Jhrh.* (1942).

[14] According to the "famous" (thus Bultmann) example of C. Holsten, *Die Christusvision des Paulus und die Genesis des paulinischen Evangelium* (1861). Also see O. Michael, *Die Entstehung der paulinischen Christologie,* ZNTW (1929), pp. 325ff; in addition also Schweitzer, *Geschichte der Paulinischen Forschung* (1933), pp. 30ff.

[15] Thus also Dibelius.

[16] Bultmann, *Neueste Paulus Forschung, op. cit.,* p. 11.

[17] Thus, for example, H. W. Beyer, *Die Apostelgeschichte* (NTD) (1947), p. 151. "These few additional words, however, enable us to get a deep insight into the pre-history of his conversion. The 'pricks' of Christ had hit the young Pharisee already before Damascus, perhaps already when he saw Stephen die. And how was it possible that the disciple of Gamaliel, the mildest, the most patient of the Pharisaical teachers, became the most ardent persecutor of the Christians? There is a breach in his inner history. And it was caused by the prick of Christ. With this prick in his heart Paul could not wait to see what this movement for Christ would become. He had to destroy it—or he would be lost in it himself. . . ."

[18] Thus Bauernfeind, *op. cit.,* p. 270, correctly states: "From this word there is simply nothing to be inferred about the time before the Damascus moment." Also Grosheide, *op. cit.* II, p. 373: the picture (of kicking against the pricks) must not be understood to mean that in his heart Paul felt something else, and did not find peace with his actions, but went against his own conscience. This does not fit the context. Paul does not speak of a turning against his better self but of an injustice which he committed. All sinful opposition against God, even if we do not recognize it as sin, is a kicking of one's heels against the pricks," cf. also Pieper, *op. cit.,* pp. 26ff.

[19] See also J. Ridderbos, *De apostel der heidenen* (1931), pp. 18ff, 273.

[20] Cf. also Lothar Schmid, TWB III, p. 666, κέντρον; this speaks of "Christ's warning to Paul against the attempt to oppose his will which would be vain and only bring harm to himself." Others as Zahn will understand σκληρόν as the inner wrestling which Paul must have undergone before surrendering to Christ's will. He speaks of "the struggle" during his three days of blindness and fasting, *Die Apostelgesch. des Lucas,* II (1927), p. 803. This appears to me to be too much the result of psychologizing. By σκληρόν nothing else is meant than that Paul set himself against Jesus, as this was revealed in his persecution of the church, and that his opposition to Jesus was fruitless and pernicious.

[21] This is naturally not to deny that Paul's conversion had a psychological aspect, and it would be interesting to know something more about this. How easy it is, however, to fall into speculation is proven, for example, by the book of O. Kietzig, *Die Bekehrung des Paulus religionsgeschichtlich und religionsphychologisch neu untersucht,* not only in its references to other opinions, but also by his own attempt to establish the "conversion-type" of Paul. Cf. pp. 72ff, pp. 101ff. F. M. Braun also points out the failure of all such attempts to explain the change in Paul's life in this manner, cf. *Jesus Christus in Geschichte und Kritik* (1950), p. 197: "After trying out various systems, a naturalistic, a psychological, a dialectical,

etc., criticism has at last condescended to admit its impotence." He appeals in this connection to statements of M. Goguel.

22 The word ἀποκαλύψαι is here of importance. Whereas φανεροῦν points more to the result, to the visible character of what is revealed, ἀποκαλύψαι lays emphasis upon the hidden quality of revelation, i.e. the disclosure of the unknown, cf. for example, H. Schlier, *Der Brief an die Galater* (in Meyer's *Kommentar*, VII (1949), p. 26.

23 For the fundamental significance of Paul's conversion for the content of his preaching of Christ, see also Leichtenhan, *Paulus* (1928), pp. 59, 60.

24 See below, Par. 12.

25 Thus, Reitzenstein, for example, *Die hellenistischen Mysterienreligionen* (1920), pp. 229ff. Also Lietzmann says that Paul here points to the divine revelation as the only possible source of his gospel. The event at Damascus hit him so very hard that he based everything that he possessed as a Christian, including his knowledge of the details of Jesus' life (as in 1 Cor. 11:23) upon the direct communication of the Lord. According to Lietzmann no matter how we may understand the situation, it must be admitted that the apostle made a factual mistake with respect to his development: "St. Paul must in any case have known about Jesus' life and about the faith of Jesus' followers through human mediation already before Damascus." *An die Galater* (1923), p. 7.

26 Cf. S. Maclean Gilmour, *Paul and the Primitive Church*, in *The Journal of Religion*, Chicago, xxv (1945), p. 122.

27 See J. Gresham Machen, *op. cit.*, pp. 47ff, also Bultmann, *Neueste Paulus-Forschung, op. cit.* (1936), p. 7.

28 See Bultmann, *op. cit.*

29 Thus Oepke describes the position of the opponents of Paul's sojourn at Jerusalem before his conversion, *Der Brief des Paulus an die Galater* (1937), p. 30.

30 Especially of importance in this connection is the fact that in these passages he calls himself a Hebrew, because this is the special characterization of the Palestinian Jews, Cf. Dibelius, *An die Philipper* (1937), p. 87 (Exkurs), and Lietzmann-Kümmel, *An Die Korinther* (1949), I-II. It is true that some groups in the Diaspora also bore this name, but probably this indicated that they had recently left Palestine. Such an interpretation would also tend to confirm the statement of Hieronymus (*De viris inlustribus* 5), that Paul's parents had immigrated from Galilean Gischala to Tarsus. In any case this name indicates the close connection between Paul and Palestinian Judaism and it confirms the statements of *Acts* that he had family in Jerusalem (23:16), and had studied there.

31 Cf. e.g., R. Leichtenhan, *Paulus*, 2nd ed., p. 44: "As this synagogue (mentioned in Acts 6:9) also embraces the Jews from Cilicia we have to seek Paul among its members, and, indeed, occupy a prominent position among those who argued with Stephan. These discussions made him acquainted with the person, the doctrine and the fate of Jesus. Cf. MacLean Gilmour, *op. cit.*, p. 126.

32 Delling describes παραλαμβάνω in 1 Cor. 11 and 15 as: "in fester

Prägung in der Traditionskette Christlicher Ueberlieferung empfangen,"
TWB IV, p. 14, and relates this to the rabbinical term. techn. "für das
Ueberkommen des Lehrinhaltes קבּל," cf. also Büchsel TWB II, p. 173, on
παραδίδωμι.

33 This is also applicable to the statement in 1 Cor. 11:23: "I have
received from the Lord." Thereby the Lord's Supper is referred to as a
human tradition, which in the last analysis goes back to the Lord (therefore
ἀπό and not παρα, that which refers to the tradition, out of whose
mouth Paul directly received this tradition). Thus Kummel, op. cit., p. 75,
is correct in his opposition to Lietzmann Idem., p. 57, who believes that
Paul here speaks of the revelation which he received from the Lord at
Damascus. See also Grosheide, op. cit., pp. 388-9. The same holds for
that matter of 1 Cor. 15:3; 7:25, where the expression "I have no command of the Lord" refers to a delivered command.

34 Cf. H. J. Holtzman, Lehrbuch des neutest, Theologie, II (1911), pp.
232ff; J. Gresham Machen, The Origin of Paul's Religion (1947) (1925),
pp. 147ff; R. Bultmann, Die Bedeutung der geschichtlichen Jesus für die
Theologie des Paulus, Glauben und Verstehen (1933), pp. 190ff; W. G.
Kummel, Jesus und Paulus, Theologische Blätter (1940), pp. 212ff.

35 Cf. A. Oepke, Die Missionspredigt des Apostels Paulus (1920), pp.
132ff.

36 C. H. Dodd, The Apostolic Preaching (1944): "We may presume
they (i.e., Peter and Paul) did not spend all the time talking about the
weather," p. 16.

37 Cf. A. Oepke, op. cit. (1920), p. 50.

38 See A. Schweitzer, Gesch. der Paulinischen Forschung (1933), p. 179,
and his Die Mystik des Apostels Paulus (1930), pp. 32ff.

39 For the present status of the discussion see also A. M. Hunter's Inter-
preting the New Testament 1900-1950 (1951), p. 72.

40 The Origin of Paul's Religion (1947), p. 129.

41 Op. cit., p. 135. Materially the same for example is the view of Floyd
V. Filson, The New Testament Against Its Environment (1950), pp. 38ff:
"The more we study the letters of Paul, the more we realize that he takes
it for granted at all times that he and the other Apostolic leaders are in
essential accord in their faith in Jesus and their thought concerning him
(Cf. Gal. 2:16; 1 Cor. 15:11). As to the law he may argue. But he
gives no hint, nor does any other New Testament writer, of a breach between himself and his fellow apostles in essential Christology."

42 Cf. J. D. Aalders, Paulus en de antieke cultuurwereld (1951), pp. 74ff;
105ff; 143ff.

43 See also Oepke, op. cit., pp. 26ff.

44 Thus Bultmann writes: "It was an historical necessity for the gospel
to be rendered in a conceptual form which was familiar to the Hellenistic
world. Such a process naturally did not take place without affecting the
contents of the gospel." Theol., p.163. Characteristic of Bultmann is the
notion of "historical necessity" and a "natural process." This statement
ought to be considered when in other passages Bultmann gives the impression

that this adaptation only concerns the "conceptual form" (*Begrifflichkeit*), thus in the discussion of the book of E. Percy, *Untersuchungen über den Ursprung der Johanneïschen Theologie*, in *Orientalistische Literaturzeitung* (1940), pp. 150-175, especially p. 152.

[45] Cf. C. Schneider, *Einführung in die Neutestamentliche Zeitgeschichte* (1934), p. 98.

[46] Cf. Oepke, *op. cit.*, pp. 88ff.

[47] The opposite appears to follow clearly at least in Paul's address on the Areopagus (Acts 17:28-29); cf. also N. B. Stonehouse, *The Aeropagus Address* (1949), pp. 23, 24, with its appeal to Calvin, although he also lays emphasis upon the antithetical character of Paul's preaching. Cf. the extensive treatment in J. H. Bavinck's *Religieus besef en Christelijk Geloof* (1949), pp. 120ff; G. C. Berkouwer's *De Algemeene Openbaring* (1951), p. 116; and J. M. Van Minnen's *Accomodatie* (1951), pp. 185ff.

[48] Reitzenstein says that one cannot call Paul the first but "the greatest of all gnostics," *Die hellenistischen Mysterienreligionen* (1920), p. 62.

[49] Reitzenstein has gone the farthest in this respect. He portrays Paul as a pneumaticus, who after his conversion went to Arabia in order there in inner experience to arrive at unshakable certainty. The tradition of the early church concerning Jesus did not interest him. He was satisfied with the confession of the church: "Jesus has died for our sins and has been raised again by God: He is the Christ" and he was satisfied with the faith that lived in the church in the pneuma, the continual revelation of Christ. "Das bot dem Manne, dem das eigene Erleben, die innere Schau Notwendigkeit war und daher Wirklichkeit wurde das Recht neben ihr alle Tradition als minderwertig zu betrachten. Das πνεῦμα θεοῦ, das doch nur eines sein kann, verbürgt die Einheit aller wahren Verkündigung und zugleich für ihn selbst die volle Freiheit . . . " Cf. *op. cit.*, p. 231, and pp. 53ff.

[50] Cf. Reitzenstein, *op. cit.*, pp. 185ff; Bousset in *Die Schriften des N.T.* II (1917), pp. 86ff.

[51] For the denial of this cf., e.g., J. Gresham Machen, *The Origin of Paul's Religion* (1947) (1925), pp. 265ff; and especially Kurt Deiszner, *Paulus und die Mystik seiner Zeit* (1921).

[52] See also F. W. Grosheide, *De eerste brief van Paulus aan de Kerk te Korinthe* (1932), p. 95, note.

[53] Thus Grosheide on 1 Cor. 2:7, *op. cit.*, p. 97, note; see also H. D. Wendland, *Die Briefe an die Korinther* (1948): "The content of the wisdom of the perfect is completely different in St. Paul's view from that of mysticism. It is the redemption through Christ at the end of time, p. 18. See Bornkamm TWB IV, pp. 825ff., cf. μυστήριον.

[54] Cf. Reitzenstein, *op. cit.*, p. 187.

[55] Kurt Deiszner, *Paulus und die Mystik seiner Zeit* (1921), pp. 22ff, Cf. also H. D. Wendland, *Die Briefe and die Korinther* (1948), p. 20, who understands the depths of God as "the mystery of divine redemption"; and Grosheide: "The concern is with the work of redemption *in concreto* and not with the impenetrable characteristics of God *in abstracto*." *Op. cit.*, p. 104.

[56] Cf. Deiszner, *op. cit.*, pp. 44ff and Wendland, *op. cit.*, p. 20: "The meaning of the gift of the Spirit is that the Christians shall be able to realize the gift of divine grace . . . the whole of God's saving activity . . . leading in Christ to the redemption, sanctification, and glorification of the faithful."

[57] Cf. Deiszner, *op. cit.*, pp. 137, 138.

[58] See the excellent work of Charles Masson, *Le Christ Jésus et l'ancien Testament selon Saint Paul* (1941) in: *Cahiers de la faculté de Theologie de l' Universite de Lausanne*, IX, of which a thankful use is made in the preceding.

[59] Masson demonstrates *op. cit.*, p. 10, that it is frequently affirmed incorrectly that for Paul the term "Christ" is simply a proper name. He points out the frequent transposition of Christ Jesus and writes: "most often and especially in the formula 'in Christ Jesus,' Paul lays emphasis on the title "Christ."

[60] From this exegesis it appears also how far Paul differs from a mystical doctrine of Christ, according to which Christ would only be the divine personification of the Pneuma. It appears here that the words "the Lord is now the Spirit," vs. 17, are based upon the historical revelation of the person of Christ, as the actual bearer of the glory of God which appeared earlier. Moreover, Christ does not here appear under the all-dominating perspective of the Pneuma, but the reverse is true, i.e., the Spirit who gives the freedom from the captivity of the law, is the Spirit of the revealed Christ, cf. also Wendland on 2 Cor. 3:17, *op. cit.*, pp. 119ff, in opposition to Bousset and others.

[61] See in addition to Masson, *op. cit.*, pp. 17ff, H. D. Wendland, *Geschichtsanschauung und Geschichtsbewusztsein im N.T.* (1938), p. 31, and the literature cited therein.

[62] *Op. cit.*, p. 16. Therefore, Masson, *op. cit.*, p. 20, believes that the problem of the New Testament in its simplest form is the problem of faith in Christ: "In reality Jesus' relation to the Old Testament ceases to be a problem when we answer the question that Jesus asks of everyone with the words: "Thou art the Christ."

CHAPTER IV

[1] Cf. also H. D. Wendland, *Der Mitte der Paulinischen Botschaft* (1935), p. 6.

[2] *Paulus* (1907), p. 72. Wrede goes so far as to say: "It is really possible to formulate the entire contents of the Pauline religion without taking any notice of the doctrine of justification except for the mentioning of the law."

[3] *Die Mystik des Apostels Paulus* (1930), p. 220. Schweitzer writes: "St. Paul uses this incidental doctrine in order to come to terms with the law from the point of view of the traditional conception about expiatory death with the aid of scriptural arguments."

[4] Cf. H. D. Wendland, *Geschichtsanschauung und Geschichtsbewusztsein*

in Neuen Testament (1938), pp. 23ff, and his *Der Mitte der Paulinischen Botschaft,* pp. 7ff, and the literature cited therein.

⁵ See also Wendland, *Geschichtsanschauung,* pp. 69ff.

⁶ See H. Ridderbos, *De Komst van het Koninkrijk* (1950), pp. 102ff.

⁷ Hereby it is not denied that this special nature of Paul's preaching is also determined by his personal experience. It was the risen and triumphant Lord who appeared to him and who also because of this encounter formed the centrum and the heart of his gospel. Cf. also Maclean Gilmour, *op. cit.,* p. 125. This will not say, however, that Paul's preaching had another content than that of those who had also known Christ in his life upon earth; it only says that Paul represents a later stadium in the progress of Christ's revelation.

⁸ Cf. Lietzmann, *An die Galater* (1923), p. 25; *An die Römer* (1933), p. 26, he writes here that thereby the adoptionist conception of Christology is excluded and that the description of the Son of God as the pre-existent one, "must be the starting-point for the understanding of this description." See also A. Oepke, *Der Brief des Paulus an die Galater* (1937), p. 74.

⁹ Thus Dibelius, *An die Thessalonicher I-II; An die Philipper* (1937), p. 77, cf. p. 73; also cf. A. Deissmann, *Paulus,* pp. 149ff.

¹⁰ Thus, e.g., W. Michaelis, *Der Brief des Paulus an die Philliper* (1935), p. 36; cf. G. Sevenster, *De Christologie van het N.T.* (1946), pp. 146ff.

¹¹ Cf. Greijdanus, *De brief van den Apostel Paulus an de Gemeente te Philipi* (1937), pp. 190-191, cf. p. 187, although according to Greijdanus, the latter presupposes the former. *Op. cit.,* p. 187.

¹² Cf. Kleinknecht. TWB II, p. 385, see εἰκών.

¹³ Grosheide's interpretation of 2 Cor. 4:4 that the conception of εἰκών refers to the material, and points therefore to the incarnation, and must be distinguished from the pre-existent equality of the Son and the Father, does not appear tenable on the basis of Col. 1:15.

¹⁴ The genitive πάσης κτίσεως, (superior to) the whole of creation, is not a genitive partit., as the Arians assumed, but it must be understood as a gen. relat. or comparative.

¹⁵ See for an extensive proof, for example, G. Sevenster, *Christologie,* pp. 144ff, and also F. M. Braun, *Jesus Christus,* pp. 191-192, and the cited schema of F. Prat, *La théologie de Saint Paul* II (1933), pp. 155ff.

¹⁶ Thus also Bultmann, *Theologie,* p. 128 and also J.A.C. Van Leeuwen, *Paulus' zendbrieven aan Efeze,* Colosse, Filémon, en Thessalonica (1926), pp. 416-417. Others translate: of our God and of the Lord Jesus Christ and consider that Christ is not here referred to as God, thus the translation of N.B.G., M. Dibelius, *An die Thessalonicher,* I, II; *An die Philipper* (1937), p. 42; A. Oepke in: *Die Kleineren Briefe des Apostels Paulus* (1949), p. 145. A strong indication for the correctness of the first conception is the lack of the article before κυρίου cf. 2 Peter 1:1, Titus 2:13.

¹⁷ Thus in addition to Bultmann, also Dibelius, *Die Pastoral briefe* (1931), p. 90. For the motivation of this conception see also C. Bouma, *De Brieven van de apostel Paulus aan Timotheus en Titus,* pp. 427, 428: J. Jeremias

146 PAUL AND JESUS

translates: "of the great God and of our Savior." He rejects the other rendering while admitting its possibility, because the description of Jesus as "the great God" would be "completely isolated and unique in the New Testament," *Die Briefe des Timotheus und Titus* (1949), pp. 59, 60; In opposition see Bouma, *op. cit.*

[18] Thus for example, also Sevenster, *op. cit.*, pp. 159-160; Greijdanus, *op. cit.*, Vol. II, pp. 410ff; E. Kühl, *Der Brief des Paulus an die Römer* (1913), pp. 315ff; Zahn-Hauck, *Der Brief des Paulus an die Römer* (1925), pp. 433ff.; E. Stauffer TWB, III, p. 106, see θεός. For the opposite meaning which assumes after the words "Christ according to the flesh," a certain pause in thought and would let the doxology proceed as follows: "the God, who is above all, be praised," etc. See, for example, W. G. Kummel, *Jesus and Paulus, op. cit.*, p. 214 and the newer literature cited therein.

[19] Thus Calvin adds: "According to the flesh, that we may understand that he has brought something superior to the flesh from Heaven: he will not have taken it from David, but he much rather derives it from the glory of the Godhead. And further by these words Paul not only ascribes the true nature of the flesh to Christ but also clearly distinguishes in them between his human and divine nature." Ed. Tholuck V. (1834), p. 3.

[20] Frequently the word σάρξ has the pregnant meaning of being in itself powerless, tarnished by sin, and subject to death. Thus Greijdanus will conceive of the phrase "according to the flesh," *op. cit.*, vol. I, pp. 60-61. κατὰ σάρκα does not need, however always to be understood in this pregnant sense, cf. Bultmann, *Theologie des N.T.* (1948), p. 233.

[21] ὁμοίωμα is here thought of concretely as the form, the form of appearance, Cf. H. Lietzmann, *op. cit.*, p. 79, with reference to Rom. 1:23; Phil. 2:7; Rev. 9:7; Ezekiel 8:2; see also Zahn, *op. cit.*, p. 382 (with reference to Tertullian who among others, translates *in simulacro,* by *in similitudinem*), Kuhl, *op. cit.*, p. 255, Greijdanus, *op. cit.* I, p. 358, and further also Schneider, TWB, V (1950), pp. 195ff.

[22] Thus Schneider, correctly opposes J. Weiss, *Das Urchristentum* (1917), pp. 376ff. Cf. also Kummel, *Jesus and Paulus, op. cit.* p. 214.

[23] See against this conception (of the Tübingers and Jülicher) Kühl *op. cit.*, p. 254. Cf. also Sevenster, *Christologie*, pp. 162ff (against Windisch).

[24] Therefore, on the one hand, ἐν ὁμοιώματι σ. ἀ. (and not simply: ἐν σαρκὶ ἁμαρτίας) yet on the other hand, also ἐ. ὁ. σαρκὸς ἁμαρτίας (and not simply: ἐν σαρκί). See also Sevenster, *op. cit.*

[25] Cf. the preceding.

[26] Especially in Lutheran theology, see, e.g., H. Bavinck, *Gereformeerde Dogmatiek III* (1929), p. 239; çf. also G. C. Berkouwer, *De Persoon van Christus* (1951), pp. 286ff.

[27] Cf. also Oepke, TWB. III, p. 661, see κενόω: "There is a strong sense of the unity of the person. The essence remains, but its mode of being is changed by it, a real sacrifice!" A much weaker position with respect to this point is taken by Schneider, in TWB. V, p. 197, with respect to ὁμοίωμα, who believes that the words in themselves permit the conclusion, "that there is nothing left of the divine essence about Him."

[28] Greijdanus writes that neither the Father nor the Son nor the Holy Spirit can detach themselves from their divine glory, which is naturally given with the fact of their being God, "they cannot empty themselves of this." But they can hide this divine glory and hide it behind something so that it does not shine through. *Op. cit.*, pp. 191-192. It appears to us that this problematic is entirely foreign to the text. When Greijdanus in the sequence writes that the Son of God did not detach himself from being God, nor did he destroy his divine glory, then this is certainly the intention of the apostle.

[29] ἐν ὁμοιώματι ἀνθρώπων γενόμενος (made in the likeness of man).

[30] While μορφή (δούλου) (the form of a servant) is opposed to μορφή (θεοῦ) (the form of God), the text is concerned with the contrast (ὁμοίωμα) ἀνθρώπων (the likeness of man) and (μορφή) θεοῦ (the form of God).

[31] Cf. also Schneider, *op. cit.*, p. 197. This appears also to be the conception of Greijdanus, *op. cit.*, pp. 193-194.

[32] This σχῆμα does not speak only of the form, the appearance, but of the action and the entrance; cf. for example Dibelius, *op. cit.*, p. 78.

[33] Cf. also Dibelius, "the elaborateness of the two expressions is intended to express the author's desire to glorify the authenticity of the humanity of the Son of God, that paradoxical miracle." *Op. cit.*, p. 81. He maintains this against a docetic interpretation of ὁμοίωμα (a likeness) and σχῆμα (fashion) (e.g., Marcion). "In contrast to such Doceticism it may be established that this passage points in the opposite direction." Cf. Michaelis, *op. cit.*, p. 38.

[34] ἐν πρώτοις (above everything) (trans. N.B.G.), "als Hauptstück" (Leitzmann adds: 'εν πρώτοις = in primis: which chiefly refers to rank,' *op. cit.* p. 76.

[35] See for example, Sevenster, *Christologie*, pp. 165ff.

[36] Cf. in addition the commentaries of Dibelius, Ewald, Van Leeuwen, and Büchsel TWB. I, p. 259, see ἀποκαταλλάσσω.

[37] The difficulty is the fact that under ἐξουσίαι and ἀρχαί Paul mostly understood evil spirits, Col. 2:15; 1 Cor. 15:24; Eph. 6:12; Rom. 8:38, but sometimes he also means good spirits, cf. Eph. 3:10; Col. 1:16 (this seems to be true in these passages). Some will therefore think of a *genus mixtum*, cf., for example, E. Lohmeyer, according to whom these powers "mean nothing but the natural determinateness of the world, including man, according to the mythical view." *Der Brief an die Kolosser*, Meyer (1930), p. 119; according to Foerster the powers represent the creation both in its divine origin, as well as in its fallen aspect. TWB. II, pp. 570ff, see ἐξουσία. All that seems to be too modern and too little *e mente Pauli*. Paul posits, on the one hand, a complete antithesis between the church and the powers, Eph. 6:12, and, on the other hand, the angels (for as such one will have to understand the powers here, cf. Strack-Billerbeck, *op. cit.*, III, p. 581) are for him elect spirits which are subject to God and serve him, 1 Cor. 13:1; 2 Cor. 11:14; Gal. 1:8, etc. In this sense one must also understand Eph. 1:21, 3:10; Cf. Phil. 2:10 and Col. 1:16.

[38] See my article, *Vrijheid en Wet in Paulus brief aan de Galaten*, in *Arcana Revelata* (1951), pp. 92-94.

148   PAUL AND JESUS

39 Also the widely held opinion that in Romans 13:1, there is this meaning of ἐξουσίαι, I consider to be unjust; there is much difference of opinion concerning 1 Cor. 2:8 (to which Bultmann repeatedly appeals in order to show Paul's dependence upon the gnostic myth), see, for example, Oepke, *Die Missions-Predigt*, p. 112. Here there is however some indication of ἄρχοντες.

40 It is characteristic that Schweitzer, for example, considers the Epistle to the Colossians to be ungenuine, *Die Mystik des Apostels Paulus* (1930), p. 43.

41 In support of this opinion he can appeal to the writing of M. Bruckner, *Die Entstehung der Paulinischen Christologie* (1903), cf. Schweitzer, *Geschichte der Paulinischen Forschung* (1933), pp. 134ff.

42 Some wish to deduce this from some specific pronouncements from the book *Enoch*. See for the pro and con of this discussion, for example, Sevenster, *Christologie*, p. 82, and the literature cited therein.

43 See par. 19.

CHAPTER V

1 Bultmann, *Glauben und Verstehen*, pp. 256-257; *Theologie*, pp. 121-124, see also pp. 52, 53. In addition Bultmann has exercised a sharp criticism of Bousset, since Bultmann conceives of the communion with Christ in Paul, not as a mystical but as an eschatological reality, that is to say, not as a vital fellowship, which lifts the initiated out of human life, but as a new possibility created in this life, which makes the faithful free from the law, from sin, and in general from the σάρξ as the sphere of the "Voorhandene," "the visible and perishable," etc. According to Bultmann Paul's preaching is not controlled by a mystical but by an existentialistic anthropology, *Glauben und Verstehen*, pp. 257ff.

2 C. H. Dodd, who writes, for example, "seldom I think has a theory been so widely accepted on more flimsy grounds." *The Apostolic Preaching* (1944), p. 15.

3 See for the following, for example, W. Foerster, *Herr ist Jesus* (1924) and from the same author the article κύριος in TWB, III, pp. 1087ff; in addition, E. Stauffer, *Theologie des N. T.* (1941), pp. 94-96; F. Büchsel, *Thologie des N.T.* (1937), p. 93, Cf. p. 192, pp. 109ff; Sevenster, *Christology*, pp. 149-158 A. M. Hunter, *The Unity of N.T.* (1946), pp. 36-37; Floyd V. Filson, *The New Testament Against Its Environment* (1950), pp. 36ff; of special significance is in my opinion still the extensive and penetrating argument of J. Gresham Machen, *The Origin of Paul's Religion* (1947) (1921), pp. 293-317.

4 Cf. Stauffer, *op. cit.*, p. 95.

5 Bultmann's, *Theologie des N.T.*, p. 52.

6 Cf. Büchsel, *op. cit.*, p. 192, sub. 5.

7 Cf. Sevenster, *op. cit.*, p. 153.

8 Cf. Stauffer, *op. cit.*, pp. 94, 95.

9 Cf. Machen, *op. cit.*, pp. 195ff.

10 *Kyrios Christos* (1921), p. 84.

11 Bultmann, *op. cit.*, pp. 52, 53.

12 Cf. K. G. Kuhn, TWB IV, p. 473, see μαραναθά.

13 Kuhn, *op. cit.*, p. 474.

14 Charles Masson has pointed this out.

15 See par. 13.

16 Certainly one must here consider the peculiar ambivalence which the name the Son of Man possesses, namely, as a description of Christ's glory according to Dan. 7, and of his human nature, which during his life upon earth, Jesus can employ in order to disclose his glory and to hide his glory, see my *Zelfopenbaring en Zelfverberging* (1946), pp. 50-51.

17 Cf. also M. Dibelius on Phil. 2:11, *op. cit.*, p. 81, "The whole passage aims at the worship of Christ, not only on the part of the church but on the part of the whole cosmos. . . . There is more that belongs to the Lord than the church alone, and in the final era, the church will be replaced by the cosmos in the rule of Christ."

18 That in the *Kyrios* title other moments are to be distinguished is naturally not to be denied. Cf. Stauffer, *op. cit.*, p. 96, and especially Sevenster, *op. cit.*, pp. 155-156.

19 Cf. A. Deissmann, *Licht von Osten* (1933), pp. 298ff.

20 Cf. Oepke, *Missionspredigt*, p. 147.

21 Thus Bultmann, *Theologie*, p. 124.

22 Cf. above par. 13.

23 Cf. also Wendland, *Die Briefe an die Korinther* (1948), p. 119: "Then, however, it is wrong to interpret St. Paul's thought as an almost mystical doctrine of the Spirit used to explain the person of Christ. St. Paul's belief in the Spirit is much rather based on his faith in Christ, and precisely in this connection it is something entirely different from the other religious doctrines of the Spirit existing in his day." Lietzmann still follows Bousset in his interpretation of 2 Cor. 3:17: "The κύριος (as a person), however, is the πνεῦμα (as substance)," *An die Korinther* I-II (1949) p. 113.

. 24 Bultmann also recognizes this in opposition to Bousset and he demonstrates that the character of the sacrament and the formula ἐν χριστω indicate the vital communion of the faithful with Christ, *Glauben und Verstehen*, p. 257.

25 For the place of the Holy Spirit in Jesus' preaching according to the synoptic gospels see H. Ridderbos, *Komst van het Koninkrijk*, p. 92, pp. 231ff.

26 Bultmann, *Theologie*, pp. 127ff.

27 We find this scheme essentially repeated in his article *Das Christologische Bekenntnis des Oekumenischen Rates*, in *Evangelische Theologie* (1951), pp. 1-13, see pp. 2-5. Including the Jewish Christian conception of the Son of God, as a messianic title, there is thus thought to be no less than four different religious historical types of Sons of God which determine the New Testament Christus-Kerugma. Moreover the other names of Christ (*Kyrios, Soter,* etc.) are thought besides to have their own religious

historical background. One here sees to what confusion one finally arrives, if one wishes to explain "the development of New Testament Christology" according to religious historical schemata. When, however, one conceives of the entire person-Christology in the New Testament as a mythological "explication," one cannot escape this fate, no matter how difficult it may be to conceive that the apostolic tradition in a short time could have been made into such a unrecognizable mixture of Jewish, Greek, and Egyptian myths, and that Paul and John could then supplement it further with Eastern *gnosis*.

28 Cf. the preceding conclusion of par. 11.

29 *Ibid.*

30 In his article *Les origines du dogme Paulinien de la divinité du Christ* in: *Revue Biblique*, XLV (1936), pp. 5-33.

31 Lagrange affirms that another conception of the Godhead of Christ is not thinkable in Paul as a monotheist. . . . "As, according to a monotheist, divine generation gives birth to the Son within the unique and eternal deity," *op. cit.*, p. 18.

32 Cf. par. 18.

33 Thus Bultmann, *Theologie*, p. 127.

34 That Judaism did not view the Messiah as a divine being can be established by a special inquiry into the sources, Cf. Strack-Billerbeck, *op. cit.* II, p. 626.

35 Cf. K. L. Schmidt, TWB III, p. 501 see ἐπικαλέω: "What the Old Testament says of the Lord (κύριος) יְהוָֹה is said of the Lord Jesus Christ in the New Testament. In a few places the object of the verb ἐπικαλεῖσθαι is God the Father: Acts 2:21; in other places, however, it is God the Son: Acts 7:59; 9, 14, 21; 22:16." Also the absolute use of "the name" points to this, because "in the language of the Rabbis it was used to denote the Most High," thus Braun, *op. cit.*, p. 186.

36 Cf. Braun, *op. cit.*, p. 186, where he quotes Cullmann: In Christology it is important to insist on a point that is usually ignored by New Testament criticism and which reminds us of Form Criticism, viz., that already the oldest original tradition recognized in Jesus the incarnate Divine Being.

37 Cf. Foerster, TWB III, p. 1094, κύριος, and Sevenster, *op. cit.*, p. 306.

38 *Op. cit.*, p. 185. See Joseph Schmitt, *Jesus ressuscité dans la prédication apostolique* (1949), pp. 175ff.

39 Cf. F. V. Filson, *The New Testament against its Environment* (1950), p. 41.

40 *Theologie*, pp. 50-51.

41 See H. Ridderbos, *Komst van het Koninkrijk* (1950), pp. 81ff.

42 For the complete summary of the text material, see for example, J. Bieneck, *Sohn Gottes als Christusbezeichnung des Synoptiker* (1951), pp. 35-44.

43 One finds this conception which is nearly universally abandoned in the writing of W. Grundmann, *Die Gottes Kindschaft in der Geschichte Jesu* (1938).

44 *Op. cit.*, pp. 27-34; 70-74. Bieneck bases his views here on the religious historical material presented by G. P. Wetter, *Der Sohn Gottes* (1916), and L. Bieler, ΘΕΙΟΣ ΑΝΗΡ, *das Bild des "göttlichen Mensen,"* in *Spätantike und Frühchristentum* I (1935).

45 In particular Bieneck points to this with an appeal to Wetter, *op. cit.*, p. 72.

46 Cf. M. Dibelius in R. G. G., I, p. 1595, see *Christologie*; F. Hauck, *Das Ev. des Lukas* (1934), p. 55; J. Schniewind, *Das ev. nach Markus* (1949), pp. 46-47.

47 Thus J. Bieneck, *op. cit.*, expresses himself. This tends apparently to the ontological conception. Cf. Th. Zahn, *Das ev. des Matth.* (1922), p. 150; F. W. Grosheide, *Het heilige Evangelie volgens Mattheüs* (1922), pp. 30ff.

48 At least according to the most commonly accepted text.

49 Bieneck is embarrassed by verse 41. He considers that even the evangelists did not have apparently the correct understanding of this claim of the demons. *Op. cit.*, p. 52. Greijdanus, who would accept vs. 41a, "in its full sense" denies what stands in 41b. *Het heilig Evangelie naar de beschrijving van Lucas I* (1940), p. 228.

50 That in the mouth of Caiaphas the title of the Son of God refers to the eternal and natural function of Christ is in general not acceptable; cf. Strack-Billerbeck, *op. cit.* I, p. 1006, III, p. 20. Therefore, Luke 22:70, is not to be conceived of in another sense than in vs. 67. See Greijdanus, *op cit.* II, pp. 1107 and 1109 and Bieneck, *op. cit.*, pp. 54-55.

51 Whereby others are still left out of view, as for example Luke 1:35, in which the Sonship of Christ apparently in view of the motivating διό is explained in terms of his conception by the Holy Spirit and thus is not applied to its pre-existence.

52 This holds in our opinion also of the confession of Peter, as clearly appears from the prohibition of Jesus, which follows this confession in all three gospels, and forbids that Peter disclose him to be the Christ (Matt. 16:20, Mark 8:29, 30, Luke 9:20-21). Also Jesus' word to Peter that flesh and blood has not disclosed this to him forms no counter instance. For to see the Christ in Jesus a divine illumination was necessary, as also appears from Matt. 13:11.

53 See in addition to that which Bieneck discloses in this connection. *Op. cit.*, pp. 24ff, also Strack-Billerbeck, *op. cit.*, III, p. 20.

54 W. Michaelis writes in his essay on "Die Christologie von Phl. 2:6-11": "In Jesus' consciousness at being the Son we shall have to see the decisive starting point of all later Christology": *Der Brief des Paulus an die Philipper* (1935), p. 45.

55 Sevenster, *op. cit.*, p. 101 and the literature cited therein, for example, also Stauffer, *Die Theol. des N.T.*, p. 94: "Both in the synoptics and in John and Paul, the concept 'Son of God' always has a two-fold sense. The Son of God has not only been anointed by God. He also comes from heaven in some form or other." In addition cf. Stonehouse, *The Witness of Matthew and Mark to Christ* (1944), pp. 211ff, 16ff; and the same author, *The Witness of Luke to Christ* (1951), pp. 166ff.

152 PAUL AND JESUS

⁵⁶ Over the so-called pre-existence pronouncements and the synoptic gospels, see the following paragraph.

⁵⁷ See par. 4.

⁵⁸ Of the literature from Bultmann's school which tries to make acceptable the gnostic interpretation of the so-called hellenistic Christianity, on specific points, cf. H. Schlier (*Christus und die Kirche in Epheser-brief* (1930)), E. Käsemann, (*Leib und Leib Christi* (1933); *Das wandernde Gottesvolk* (1938)); H. W. Bartsch, *Gnostisches Gut und Gemeinde-Tradition bei Ignatius von Antiochien* (1940). See also *Theol. Rundschau* N.F. (1936), pp. 18ff; *Orientalistische Literaturzeitung* (1940), p. 151.

⁵⁹ Cf. *Das Urchristentum* (1949), p. 218ff; *Theologie*, pp. 174ff.

⁶⁰ *Theologie*, pp. 164ff.

⁶¹ Bultmann, *Orient. Literaturzeitung* (1940), p. 151.

⁶² H. Lietzmann, *Geschichte der alten Kirche* I (1932), p. 33. Lietzmann has extensively treated this question in *Ein Beitrag Zur Mandäerfrage*, SBA (1930), pp. 596-608. See for the so-called *Mandäerfrage*, in addition to the views of Baumgartner (see note 63). See also the orientating writing of J. Behm, *Die mandäische Religion und das Christentum* (1927); with respect to the closely connected pre-Christian Jewish (Dead Sea) sect that is again the center of attention, see, for example, A. Dupont-Sommer, *Observations sur le Commentaire d'Habacuc, decouvert près de la Mer Morte* (1950), pp. 24ff.

⁶³ This is also admitted by those who considered the later New Testament authors to be dependent upon the Mandean gnosis. Bultmann recognizes that no New Testament writings can be shown to be dependent upon any Mandean text while the Mandean literature displays dependence upon the syncretistic Manicheans and the (Christian) Nestorians. However, there are various new authors that accept the Western (Palestinian) origin of the Mandeans, cf. W. Baumgartner, *Der heutige Stand der Mandäerfrage, Theol. Zeitschrift,* (Basel) (1950), pp. 401ff. Others, however, lay the emphasis upon the Babylonian origin. From all this it appears that the genealogy of Mandeanism is very uncertain, Baumgartner, *op. cit.,* pp. 409-410.

⁶⁴ G. Percy, *Untersuchungen über den Ursprung der johanneischen Theologie* (1939), pp. 291-292. Cf. also the same author, *Die Probleme der Kolosser und Epheserbriefe* (1946), pp. 112ff.

⁶⁵ Cf. the above par. 4.

⁶⁶ *Untersuchungen*, p. 290.

⁶⁷ In this respect Bultmann recognizes that Percy, "has adduced a great deal of what is correct in opposition to a number of hasty hypotheses, and I (i.e., Bultmann) am not in a position to say anything decisive about it." *Orient. Literaturzeitung* (1940), p. 173.

⁶⁸ J. Jeremias, *Theol. Blätter* (1940), p. 277.

⁶⁹ *Oriental. Lit-Zeitung* (1940), p. 166.

⁷⁰ *Ibid.,* p. 169.

⁷¹ Therefore, it appears to us that the attempt to derive Paul's doctrine

of pre-existence from the idea of the pre-existent Son of Man, which occurs in some Jewish apocalypses (especially in the manner of M. Brückner, *Entstehung der paulinischen Christologie* (1903), is a misunderstanding of the revelatory character of Pauline Christology. What Paul preaches concerning Christ's Deity, his exaltation, and pre-existence, rests for him not upon any theological speculation, but upon the impact of that which was revealed to him concerning Christ as the living Lord, the Son of God. Paul was no historian of religion, he was a witness of revelation. This in opposition to O. Michel, *Die Entstehung der paulinischen Christologie*, ZNTW (1929), pp. 329ff.

[72] Thus, also Bultmann, *Die Geschichte der synoptischen Tradition* (1931), pp. 168ff, also pp. 165ff. He refers here for clarification to gnostic texts.

[73] See also the strong argument of G. Sevenster, *op. cit.,* pp. 102-105.

[74] Cf. Percy, *Untersuchungen,* p. 202.

[75] See above, end of par. 6.

[76] J. Gresham Machen, *The Origin of Paul's Religion,* p. 312.

[77] Cf. par. 15.

[78] Thus also E. Stauffer, *Die Theologie des N.T.* (1945): "By calling himself the Son of Man, Jesus lay claim to the decisive position in universal history," p. 92.

[79] Cf. above par. 16.

[80] *Theologie,* p. 171.

[81] See, for example, A. J. Festugière, *L' idéal religieux des Grecs et l'Evangelie* (1932), pp. 161ff and *passim.*

[82] Cf. Dibelius, *An die Kolosser* (1927), pp. 9ff; Bultmann, *Theologie,* p. 131.

[83] The Hermetic writings (Corpus Hermeticum) are a collection of the writings written in Greek which derive their name from *Hermes Trismegistos,* the Egyptian god, Thot. Their content is a mixture of religious mysticism and cosmological speculations. Their origin, in their present form, lies in the third and fourth centuries after Christ.

[84] Dibelius, *op. cit.*

[85] Cf. par. 18.

[86] Thus, for example, Dibelius: "Without the need of adducing more examples it is clear that St. Paul puts his Christ in the position of the κόσμος of the Hermetic writings, the κόσμος νοητός-λόγος of Philo, of the original man of the 'Iranian' texts." *Op. cit.,* p. 11. Masson observes: "Nevertheless it is a little surprising to have to state that men like M. Dibelius, and before him John Weiss, talk without a blush or a quiver about 'Christ as the world-soul and creator of the world' in connection with Col. 1:16. They do not notice that in order to account for this aspect of St. Paul's theology they have resource to conceptions entirely foreign to him." *L'Epitre de Saint Paul aux Colossians* (1950), p. 108.

[87] Thus, for example, also Sevenster, *Christologie,* p. 148 and Büchsel, *Theologie,* p. 114, see also A. D. Galloway, *The Cosmic Christ* (1951), p. 51.

[88] See in particular also the article of H. Windisch, "Die göttiche Weisheit der Juden" in *N.T. Studien für Henrici* (1914), pp. 220-245, in which this conception finds its most detailed defense.

[89] The Septuagint has: κύριος ἔκτισεν με ἀρχὴν ὁδῶν αὐτοῦ εἰς ἔργα αὐτοῦ.

[90] LXX, ἤμην παρ' αὐτῷ ἁρμοζόυσα.

[91] Cf. F. Delitzsch, *Das salomon. Spruchbuch* (1873), p. 147; Büchsel, *op. cit.*, p. 115.

[92] προτέρα πάντων ἔκτισται σοφία.

[93] ἡ πάντων τεχνῖτις.

[94] ἀτμίς.

[95] ἀπόρροια.

[96] ἀπαύγασμα.

[97] εἰκών.

[98] τὴν των σων θρόνων πάρεδρον σοφίαν.

[99] Windisch, *op. cit.*, pp. 225, 243, believes that this identification of Jesus Christ with the Biblical figure of Wisdom was decisive for the deification of Jesus, p. 23.

[100] It is true that some will consider the Old Testament and late Jewish pronouncements concerning Wisdom to be dependent upon pagan conceptions, especially those of the Iranian texts concerning the primeval man. Thus, for example, Dibelius, *op. cit.*, p. 11, Cf. also Bultmann, *Theologie*, p. 131. It is, however, necessary to realize how great the distance between this "primeval man" that is to say the macrocosmic man, who as a sort of collective world soul, is present in everything, and that which is said in Proverbs concerning Wisdom, which before the creation of the world, was with God. In addition there is between the Old Testament and the Iranian conception of the origin of the world a tremendous difference. See also Percy, *Die Probleme der Kolosser und Epheserbriefe* (1946), p. 69; Büchsel, *Theologie*, p. 200.

[101] Windisch has tried to demonstrate this by showing the connection between that which is said in the Enoch about the Son of Man and Proverbs 8 about Wisdom. *Op. cit.*, p. 227. Again all this is very speculative. Nowhere does there appear anything of an identification of the Messiah with Wisdom.

[102] Thus Percy, *Probleme*, p. 70.

[103] Cf. e.g., Strack-Billerbeck, *op. cit.* II, pp. 353-358; III, pp. 129-131, and Kittel, TWB IV, pp. 139ff. see, λέγω.

[104] In order to come under this impression one must read the related passages in Proverbs, Jesus Sirach, and Sapientia in context. The danger is always present that the similarity is thought to be present because of single expressions which are selected and that one does not give sufficient emphasis to the total character of the text by which they are determined. In the preceding we have therefore cited much more than for example that which is cited by Windisch. The result is that the apparent agreement is much less evident!

[105] See Percy, *Probleme*, p. 71: "Above all it seems very doubtful to me

whether the conception of Jesus as the Mediator of Creation could only be derived from identifying Him with wisdom or a similar figure, if the belief in Christ as such had not offered some starting point for such a belief." And Masson, *op. cit.*, p. 101: "This certainly has too directly proceeded from the revelation in Christ, and its expression is too simple for it to be derived from speculations about the wisdom of this world," even though this author will not deny the possibility of a certain connection with Prov. 8.

[106] Commonly men point for what the Old Testament says to Gen. 1:27, thus, for example, Kittel, TWB. II, p. 394, see εἰκών; and Grosheide, on 2 Cor. 4:4. In any case the radiation of God's glory, which is mentioned in Col. 1:16 and 2 Cor. 4:4, is other than that of the original or of the new man. It has in the first place a relationship to Christ's divine glory and activity. For the doctrine of man as the image of God, one can, in our opinion, not appeal to these passages, at least not directly.

[107] Cf. H. Lehmann, "Schöpfergott und Heilsgott im Zeugnis des Bibel" in *Evangelische Theol.* (Sept., 1951), p. 108, in exposition of John 1, Col. 1: "Consequently, Christ is the origin, and the goal of cosmic history. This is to say: Christ is not to be understood from the creation, but the creation is to be understood from Christ—and in its relation to Christ." In our opinion this is a false contrast. Cf. Berkouwer, *De algemeene openbaring* (1951), pp. 251ff.

[108] Insofar as I can see it is never said in the New Testament that the Father has created the world by the Son as it is said that the world is redeemed by him, etc. See Col. 1:20ff.

[109] One compares, for example, the πρωτότοκος πάσης κτίσεως (gen. comp. not part.!) in Col. 1:15 with ἔκτισεν με in Proverbs 8 and Sirach 1. In addition in Col. 1 Christ is the *subject* of ἔκτισεν, which is never said of Wisdom. Also the very inclusive τὰ πάντα ἐν αὐτω συνέστηκεν lacks any parallel in the wisdom pronouncements.

524122